MERSEY DOCKS
FLEET LIST
1850 - 1980

Compiled by
Gordon F. Wright

Published for
LIVERPOOL NAUTICAL RESEARCH SOCIETY
2006

First Published 2006 for the Liverpool Nautical Research Society
by Countyvise Limited, 14 Appin Road, Birkenhead, Wirral CH41 9HH.

The author has made every reasonable effort to contact all copyright holders. Any errors/omissions that may have occurred are inadvertent and regretted, and anyone who, for any reason, has not been contacted is invited to write to the publishers so that full acknowledgement may be made in subsequent editions of this work.

British Library Cataloguing in Publication Data.
A catalogue record for this book is available from the British Library.

Please note: From 1st January 2007 ISBNs will contain 13 numbers these numbers will be the same as the present number printed below the barcode (ie. starting 978).
Countyvise is showing both existing (10 digit) and future (13 digit) ISBNs on the Title page verso. Please continue to use the 10 figure number until 31st December 2006.

ISBN 1 901231 66 6   ISBN 978 1 901231 66 3

Mersey Docks and Harbour Board dredger - Walter Glynn

BRIEF HISTORY

It is not often realised that the current Mersey Docks Company is the successor to a concern that is almost 300 years old. Gordon Wright spent seven years researching the floating units of the Mersey Docks & Harbour Board expecting to find about 200 or so vessels, in fact he has listed 366 vessels of all sizes from about 2 tons to 4,000 tons: from 10 feet in length to over 400 ft. An astonishing fleet.

These vessels were acquired in order to service the navigation of the Mersey and its surrounding waters, survey and chart them. In 1831 Lt Denham had the task of surveying and producing a chart of the entrances to the Estuary. This he did and found another new channel, a more favourable waterway. In 1838 he attempted to remove a new sandbar using a couple of bucket dredgers and also using a method of harrowing the sandy bottom just after high water, - sand, so disturbed, was carried away by the swift flowing ebb tide, with indefinite results.

From 1709-1811 the Corporation of Liverpool acted as Trustees managing the docks by a committee appointed from their own body. In 1811 the Corporation were created a corporate body under the title of "Trustees of the Liverpool Docks". The committee was made up of 21 members of the Corporation.

In 1825, though the trust remained the same, the constitution of the committee was changed by the inclusion of eight members elected by the Dock Ratepayers, the remaining thirteen members being members of and elected by the common council who, in turn, appointed the chairman from one of the thirteen. By an act of 1851 the Committee was altered to consist of twenty four members, twelve appointed by the Council from their own body, twelve by the Dock Ratepayers, the chairman being elected by the committee from the twelve council members, the power of veto remaining with the Trustees.

In 1855 The Corporation of Liverpool purchased from the Birkenhead Trustees and Birkenhead Dock Company the property in the Birkenhead Docks for £1,143,000. In 1857 as a consequence of a bill promoted by the Manchester Chamber of Commerce, the Manchester Commercial Association and The Great Western Railway, The Mersey Docks & Harbour Board was constituted, paying the Liverpool Corporation £1,143,000 in respect of the Birkenhead Docks and £1,500,000 for the town and anchorage dues. The first meeting of the Mersey Docks & Harbour Board was held on January 5th 1858.

As the age of steam and iron dawned, the Mersey Board was faced with a choice - either sink down to a lost port like the silted harbours of Suffolk, or to grasp the nettle and invest vast sums in modernising the port facilities. It chose, of course, the latter.

A great matter of concern at this time was the depth of water at dock entrances, vessels drawing only nineteen feet were unable to dock immediately they arrived, those drawing twenty four feet could enter on very few days of the year. During the first six months of 1857, 112 vessels had been held up in the river through lack of sufficient water. In 1860 there were seven recognized channels: Formby, Crosby, Zebra, Horse, Queen's, Rock, Victoria, into the Mersey. Several of these had little water at low tide, although there would be over twenty feet of water at even the lowest of high tides. But there were delays of several hours for many of the larger mail/passenger liners.

Throughout the earlier campaign for the Manchester Ship Canal, great play had been made of the fact that the Dock Board had not dredged the Bar. The increasing size of the passenger liners, the rivalry between the liner companies and the ever more insistent demand for speed led Mr. Ismay and others to urge more and more vigorously the deepening of the Bar.

The following is an extract of a letter dated 26th October 1886 from Mr. T. H. Ismay of the White Star Line to the Chairman of the Board:

The continued pre-eminence of the Port of Liverpool, is a subject of such vital importance to one whose business is centred here as to afford sufficient excuse for my addressing you upon some matters which have a material bearing upon the future prosperity of the Port. It will not be necessary to remind your Board, of the growing necessity for building vessels of increased size and deeper draught.

Unfortunately Liverpool is very heavily handicapped by the formidable Bar at the mouth of the Mersey, which during a great part of every day throughout the year compels the majority of the vessels that now enter or leave the river to wait in many cases for several hours until there is sufficient depth of water to allow them to cross. I venture therefore to suggest that the present is an opportune time to adopt measures for dealing in earnest with the Bar outside Liverpool and if not remove it altogether at any rate by a well devised system of dredging assisting the natural forces and therefore considerable lessening it. Scarcely second in importance to the deepening of the Bar is the question of converting Liverpool into a Free Port for produce by levying upon ships the dues now collected on articles of import and export.

In 1890 a very considerable decision was taken. It was to fit up two hoppers with sand pump dredging equipment to work on the Bar. The first one (No.7) commenced work 15th September 1890 and the second (No.5) in April 1891. In 1893 when the S.P.D. BRANKER came into commission over 2,400,000 tons had been dredged, a year later the figure was 6,846,000 tons.

Before many years were past, pilots and navigators were expressing concern at the distortion of the Queens and Crosby channels by the forward movement of Askew Spit with the simultaneous growth of Taylor's Spit. By the end of the century the width of the channel was becoming affected. The problem became acute from 1903 onwards and led to the consideration of the various schemes for revetting the face Taylor's Bank to arrest its erosion and to stop the channel going to the North.

There was a strong feeling amongst practical men that the deposit of sand by the sand pump dredgers, which had now become so prominent a part of the Port's life, in the gut across the Burbo Bank, at that time lying between C.8 and C.10 red buoys, was responsible for the protrusion of the Spit.

On November 3rd 1905, Mr.Lyster (Chief Engineer) reported that, in his judgement:

This growth had nothing whatever to say to the deposit of sand by the various suction dredgers, but that it was the normal and simple phenomenon which appears in and is inseparable from all cases of bends in rivers, the concave side of the river being invariably deep and the opposite or convex side being shallow. He did advise the revetting of the Taylors Bank on the opposite side of the channel with stone brought from Welsh quarries by hopper barges and dumped along the margin of the bank

After many consultations by the Board with a group of eminent engineers, they concurred generally with Mr. Lyster. Their final opinion was given on 19th October 1906. By March 1907 the Board were able to announce two things: first, they had decided to build the revetment, to which the authority of the Acting Conservator and the Lords of the Admiralty had been obtained, and second, that they were about to construct a dredger of three times the size and power of their existing sand pumps. This was to be the famous LEVIATHAN of 10,000 tons capacity. The vessel was built at Cammel Laird & Co. launched in October 1908 and started work in 1909. There had been feeling in some minds that, despite what had been said by the consultants as to the dredging of Askew Spit,

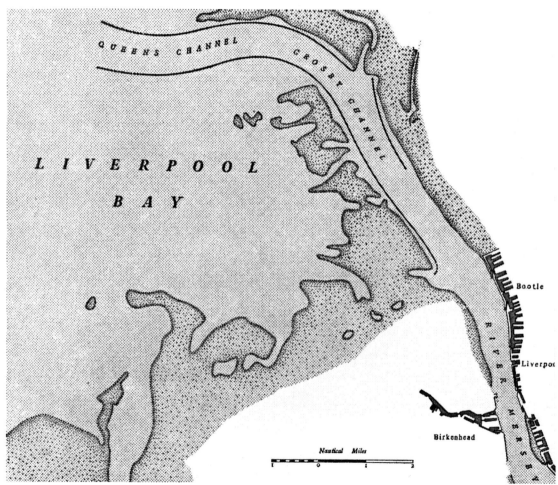

Chart of Entrance Channels, showing revetments etc

6

the LEVIATHAN should be tried out at this place. There were obvious misunderstandings concerning the use of the vessel but Mr. Lyster maintained throughout that it would be wrong and indeed impracticable to use the great dredger on Askew Spit, at least until the revetment was built. Her proper function was to deepen the main channel. Dredging on the Spit was, however, decided upon and other craft proceeded with the work.

Work on Taylor's Bank revetment commenced in May 1909 and was completed in 1910. Many years later consultants then advising the Board were of the opinion that it was a great pity that the work had not started much earlier when erosion was first noticed as a 'wandering' of the channels might then have been avoided.

By 1912 and probably much earlier it had become obvious to the experts that the Taylor's Bank Revetment was but a start of a comprehensive scheme of Training Banks. Later it became evident that dredging alone could not maintain suitable depths in certain parts of the channels. So, towards the end of 1922, the Board authorised the construction of further walls along the buoyed channels, Ingeniously concentrating and guiding the flow of the tides themselves to increase scour. The completed programme would involve nearly twenty miles of embankment.

DREDGING

REPORT FROM 1905.

Some years ago the Bar which extended across the entrance of the main channel leading to the Port became a matter of concern. There was generally ample depth of water in the channel itself on all conditions of the tide, but at the Bar at dead low water, spring tides, there was only about 11 feet of water. The consequence was that, upon arrival at the Bar, vessels drawing over 10 feet of water had to wait for the tide to rise. As the size and tonnage of vessels using the Port gradually increased the Mersey Docks & Harbour Board decided to make an attempt to dredge the channel across the Bar.

The work was commenced in July 1890, and two of the Boards ordinary steam hopper barges (No's 5 & 7) were fitted up with centrifugal sand pumps, the suction tube of No.5 being 18 inches in diameter, and that of No.7. 22 ins. These vessels were capable of filling their own hoppers with sand in about half-an-hour. The result of this work being successful, the Board in 1892 decided to have a new hopper dredger built, this vessel, which was larger than any hitherto built, was named BRANCKER, after one of the Chairmen of the Mersey Board and cost over £60,000.

The BRANCKER, 320 ft. long, 45.5 ft. beam and a draught of 19.4 ft. and having a hopper capacity for about 3,000 tons, commenced work in July 1893. This dredger fills itself in varying times, according to the quality of the material, the minimum time being about 25 minutes. It has dredged as much as 39,000 tons of sand within 24 hours and 183,000 in one week of 5½ days. In November 1895, a duplicate of the BRANCKER, the G.B.CROW (named after the current Chairman of the Boards Marine Committee, 1905) was put to work on the Bar, and another dredger of the same type was put on at the beginning of 1904, this last mentioned dredger is the

CORONATION and is of the twin screw self propelling pattern, with a hopper capacity of about 70,000 cubic feet. As the CORONATION performed her work so successfully an order was given to Messrs Ferguson Bros. of Port Glasgow, for another large dredger, called VULCAN.

This vessel, launched 11th October 1904, is 207 ft. long, with a moulded depth of 41 ft., and is capable of dredging 10,00 tons per hour from 56 ft. below the water level. The design of the dredger embodies several special features, was prepared by the builders to meet the requirements of the Mersey Board for deep dredging in hard material and working close to the dock and quay walls. The bucket ladder projects in advance of the hull for a distance sufficient to enable the vessel to dredge up to the dock walls when the buckets are lowered.

The vessel has been built throughout under Lloyd's special survey to class 100 A1. The hull is subdivided into 14 watertight compartments. Side shoots are arranged for discharging the dredge material over either side of the vessel into hopper barges, the lifting and lowering of each shoot being worked by an independent engine. The regulation of the dredging to either side of the vessel is controlled by a strong flap valve door fixed at the apex of the shoots and worked by gear from the main deck. Steam steering gear is fitted at the end of the engine casing, controlled from the wheelhouse, situated at the top of the main gear framing. A complete installation of electric is fitted throughout the vessel, large arc lamps being placed on the deck for night work. The main engines, which are employed for either propelling the vessel, or driving the dredging gear, consist of two sets of triple expansion engines capable of indicating 1,250 hp. The dredger buckets and links are of a special strong design, each bucket having a capacity of 21 cubic feet. A large steam crane is fitted on the deck for overhauling the buckets and links and for general purposes. Power steam winches are also fitted at the bow and stern for manipulating the mooring chains and holding the dredger.

Bucket Ladder Dredgers Workings.

Always one at Brunswick entrance and one at (Old) Canada Dock entrance most times One seemed to alternate between Alfred entrance and the old Princes entrance. Except for Brunswick, grab hoppers were employed for the dredging of river entrances.

September 9th 1955.

200,000 tons of stone had been required to complete North Training Wall and 460,000 tons of stone required for topping up existing wall.

THE PILOTAGE SERVICE OF 1905.

The pilotage service of the port is now worked by steam vessels, though formerly it was worked by sailing schooners, and there are now (1905) four of these steam pilot boats at work on the three pilot stations outside the port viz:- Bar, Point Lynas and Puffin Island. Pilotage - save for coasting vessels in ballast or under 100 tons burden is compulsory for all vessels. Inward bound vessels must pick up a pilot off the Anglesey coast, but outward vessels are only required to be piloted as far as the Bar.

In 1897 the Mersey Docks & Harbour Board, who are the Pilotage Authority for the port, instituted a series of form and colour tests for their pilots, a step which was indicative of their desire to have the Mersey Pilotage Service as safe and reliable as possible. All masters, mates etc. who hold Pilotage Certificates for the port are required, by the Merchant Shipping Act, 1894, to contribute so much towards the Pilotage Fund of the district, both on receiving their Pilotage Certificate, And on renewing same.

LIGHTHOUSES, LIGHTSHIPS ETC. 1905

The Mersey Docks & Harbour Board are also entrusted with the lighting etc. of the approaches to the Port, and so maintain an excellent lighthouse and lightship service. The lightships are moored as follows, one opposite Crosby, one opposite Formby, one near the Bar and one some eight miles N.W. of the Bar Lightship, called the North West Lightship.

It will be seen that these lightships are in the sea channels, which are used by a fleet of between 45 to 50 thousand vessels every year, so the necessity for lightships and buoys will at once be seen.

There are two lighthouses at the mouth of the River Mersey, the North Wall Lighthouse on the Liverpool side of the river! and the Perch Rock Lighthouse, Built on the Cheshire shore! where shore and river meet. Another lighthouse which helps to light the approaches to the port, is the Bidston Lighthouse, situated inland on a hill of the same name. Its light is visible over the eastern section of the Liverpool Bay for a distance of 25 miles. The Leasowe Lighthouse is also used in conjunction with the river and Bidston lighthouses, and is visible for a radius of over 15 miles. Other lighthouses also the property of the Mersey Docks & Harbour Board are the Lower Hoylake, Dove Beacons and Crosby Lighthouse. At the southern end of the dock estate at Liverpool a light is exhibited, which, in conjunction with the Otterspool Lighthouse, marks the entrance to the channel communicating with the Upper Mersey.

1939 -1945 War Casualties

1940 - 1941

LYSTER BLD

Aug. 18th. 1940 in NW Brunswick Dock, from near miss, capsized and sank. Salvage operations commenced immediately but were suspended owing to destruction of salvage gear by further enemy action (incendiary & high explosive bombs) on Oct. 6th.1940. Salvaging recommenced June 1942.

NO.9 SHB

Dec. 22nd. 1940 in Langton branch dock sunk from a near miss, salvaged and repaired.

MAMMOTH   Floating Crane.

March 12th. - 13th, 1941 sunk by direct hits (2 bombs) in N West Float, salved and repaired.

HERCULES   Floating Crane.

May 1941 sunk in Langton Dock, direct hit by bomb, raised and repaired.

NO.20. SHB.

May 1941 in No.2 Huskisson, burnt out and sunk, raised and converted to salvage vessel, renamed WATCHFUL.

SURVEYOR No.3.

May 1941 sunk in NE Albert Dock, constructive total loss, raised and broken up.

SIRIUS   Light Vessel.

May 1941 bow blown off and sunk in SE Albert Dock, raised and removed to Tranmere Beach.

CAMEL NO.4 Salvage Lighter.

May 1941 in SW Albert Dock, damaged and leaking removed to dry dock with aid of salvage pumps and repaired.

MERSEY DOCKS & HARBOUR BOARD - FLEET LIST

NAME OFF. No	GROSS NET	BUILT	DATE	SERVICE IN MD&HB
WELLINGTON 2377	82.0	Liverpool Mottershead & Hayes	1815	Mersey flat, wood, rigged for pile-driving, working in the docks and river Reg. to the Trustees of Liverpool Docks 21.5.1831, trans. to MD&HB 1930 vessel broken up; reg. closed 3.12.1930
FENDER 1417	--	Liverpool Roger Fisher 51.0 x 15.0 x 8.3	1855	Sloop, wood, Reg to Trustees of L'pool Docks, 16.3.1855. Title of owners changed to MD&HB 5.8.1869. Sold to Wm.Avis of L'pool 5.11.1869. Sold to R.Walsh of L'pool 19.1.1870. Sold to R.Latchford, L'pool 20.1.1870. vessel lost between Blasquets & Brandon Head 11.7.1874.
CHESTER 2378	41.0	Chester	1828	Flat, wood. Reg. to Trustees of Liverpool Docks, used for carrying stores and chains between L'pool and B'head under tow. Sold to J. Hornby & Sons, Holywell for £5. 10.10.1930
MARY GOLDWORTHY 51090	55.0	Ulverston	1865	Wherry, wood, carrying flat. Sold 26.11 .1934.
ADVENTURE 76378	133.0	Liverpool W.H.Potter & Co	1875	Lump, Iron. MD&HB 14.12.1876. vessel broken up. Reg. closed 6.7.1933
ENTERPRISE 76379	133.0	Liverpool W.H. Potter & Co. 72.3 x 25.3 x 8.9	1876	Barge, iron. Wrecked & became total loss near Whitehaven Reg. closed 22.3.1916. Re-reg. as a camel 3.11.1917. Broken up at New Ferry 1933, reg. closed 6.7.1933
QUEEN 76376	83.84	Liverpool 74.0 x 17.3	1840	Light-vessel, wood, schooner. MD&HB 14.12.1876. Converted to watch vessel. Sold to J.A.Kellit, of L'pool, 16.4.1908. Reg. closed 17.11.1923
ALBERT 76370	85.6	Liverpool 71.0 x 18.8	1840	Light Vessel, wood. MD&HB 14.12.1876. Sold to W.C.Bustard of L'pool 26.1.1903, Converted to steamer
MERSEY 76372	76.0	Liverpool 71.0 x 17.8	1855	Sailing dandy, Wood. MD&HB 14.12.1876. Sold to Barrington & Jensen L'pool 6.9.1904, and converted to steamer.
ALERT 29992	172.0 87.0	Birkenhead. Laird Bros 117.8 x 21.0x 10.7 2 x 2 cyl. engs. 70hp. builders	1865	Iron, steam tender, Paddles. Sold to J. Constant, London, 22.5.1906 Sold to Jones, Foster, Burgess & Perry, engines removed converted to a lighter Sold to Barge Alert Co. 13.11.1930, Sold to L'pool Lighterage Co. Ltd. 1.12.1958 renamed SHINING STAR17.1.1960 Vessel broken up 1969. Reg. Closed 22.5.1969

Prince

Pottinger

Oak

Planet

CONSERVATOR 76371	78.08	Birkenhead Thos. Brassey & Co.	1872	Lump, iron. MD&HB 14.12.1876. Converted to DUMMY BARGE No.4 24.12.1914
ORION 76375	175.75	Liverpool W.H.Potter & Co. 103.0 x 21.2	1873	Lightship, iron. MD&HB 14.12.1876 Converted to watch vessel 1915. Renamed MARKER 31.5.1934 - name required by Orient Line for new passenger vessel Sold to Forth Barge Co L'pool 30.10.1950
PERSEVERANCE 76376 78.0		Birkenhead Thos. Brassey & Co 75.5 x 16.3 x 7.5	1872	Lump, Iron. MD&HB 14.12.1876. Converted to DUMMY BARGE No.5 16.2.1914
PRINCE 76376	170.0	Birkenhead Laird Bros	1842	Lightship, iron, schooner . MD&HB 14.12.1876. Converted to watch vessel 1899 Converted to grab dredger. Sold to W. Cooper & sons 29.3.1927 Broken up, reg. closed 27.9.1961
SIRIUS 76403	176.22	Liverpool Patton & Hodgkinson 103.3 x 21.3	1873	Lightship, iron. MD&HB 18.1.1877. Bombed and sunk May 1941 in SE Albert Dock Raised & removed to Tranmere beach & broken up. Reg closed 25.1.1944
SANDEEL 76417	42.35	Runcorn	1850	Sailing flat, wood MD&HB 20.2.1877. Vessel abandoned at Birkenhead 1914 removed and broken up. Reg. closed 26.4.1929
CROWN & ANCHOR 76418 52.76		69.0 x 17.0 x 6.85		Sailing flat, wood. Reg to MD&HB 20.2.1877. Wrecked Formby Point. Reg. closed 4.10.1902
LADY SALE 76419	44.75	Liverpool 59.4 x 16.2 x 7.5	1845	Sailing flat, wood. Reg. to MD&HB 20.2.1877. Sold 26.1.1934 & broken up. Reg. Closed 4.5.1934
MASTIFF 76420	28.0	Liverpool 48.7 x 15.0x 6.85	1835	Sailing flat, wood. Reg. to MD&HB 20.2.1877, vessel broken up. Reg. closed 30.3.1915
HALKIN 76421	20.0	--- 47.6 x 12.5 x 6.5		Divers flat, wood. Reg. to MD&1lB 20.2.1877. Converted to a hulk Reg. closed 19.7.1905
POTTINGER 76422	44.69	Liverpool 60.3 x 16.4 x 7.05	1845	Sailing flat, wood. Reg. to MD&HB 20.2.1877. Broken up by T..Shaw & Son on Tranmere Beach 28.2.1934. Reg closed 22.2.1935
SIDNEY 76423	39.54	61.5 x 17.2 x 7.05		Sailing flat, wood, Reg. to MD&HB 20.2.1877 vessel broken up Reg. closed 19.2.1916
TERRIER 76424	39.54 45.25	Liverpool 53.1 x 19.3 x 7.25	1845	Sailing flat, wood. Reg. to MD&HB 20.2.1877 Vessel broken up. Reg. closed 20.11.1929

BULLDOG 76425	46.69	Liverpool 53.1 x 19.3 x 7.25	1846	Scraping flat, wood. Reg. to MD&HB 20.2.1877 vessel broken up Reg. closed 20.11.1929
BETSEY 76426	49.0	Liverpool 65.4 x 16.9 x 6.9	1825	Derrick flat, wood. Reg. to MD&HB 20.2.1877 Vessel broken up. Reg. closed 17.10.1927
CANADA 76427	62.3	Liverpool 75.0 x 20.6 x 5.5	1828	Derrick flat, wood. Reg. to MD&HB 20.2.1877 Vessel broken up. Reg. closed 18.4.1955
GEORGE 76428	48.55	Liverpool 65.8 x 16.8 x 6.65		Sailing flat, wood. Reg. to MD&HB 20.2.1877. Wrecked at Dinorban, Anglesey 16.6.1908 Reg. closed 25.6.1908
MILO 76429	58.5	Liverpool 64 x 20.5 x 6.5	1845	Derrick flat, wood, Reg. to MD&HB 20.2.1877. Sold for scrap 13.4.1934. Reg. closed 28.6.1934
SPITFIRE 76430	59.4	Liverpool 67.3 x 18.4 x 6.5	1828	Derrick flat, wood, Reg. to MD&HB 20.2.2877. Stripped of mast, derrick & machinery, sold to J.Johnson & Son Tranmere, 1932. Reg. closed 8.11.1932
H.No. 1 76431	55.8	51.0 *x* 18.4		Scraping flat, wood, Reg. to MD&HB 20.2.1877. Vessel broken up. Reg. closed 21.1.1914
H.No. 2 76432	52.55	49.4 x 18.8		Mud barge, wood, N.R., Reg. to MD&HB 20.2.1877. Vessel broken up. Reg. closed 30.3.1896
H.No. 3 76433	48.57	50.2 x 18.0		Mud barge, wood, N.R., Reg. to MD&HB 20.2.1877 Vessel broken up. Reg. closed 30.3.1929
H.No. 4 76434	67.36	51.3 x 20.1		Divers flat, wood, Reg. to MD&HB 20.2.1877 Vessel broken up. Reg. closed 30.3.1907
H.No. 5 76435	50.72	50.2 x 18.3		Scraping flat, wood, Reg. to MD&HB 20.2.1877 Vessel broken up. Reg. closed 30.3.1913
H.No. 6 76436	57.59	52.1 x 18.8		Mud barge, wood, N.R., Reg. to MD&HB 20.2.1877 Vessel broken up. Reg. closed 13.11.1895
H.No. 7 76437	64.1	52.3 x 20.6 x 6.15		Mud barge, wood, N.R., Reg. to MD&HB 20.2.1877. Reg. closed 21.11.1913, re-reg'd 16.1.1914 as DUMMY BARGE No.3 for use at Princes Stage. Broken up, reg. closed 12.6.1919
H.No. 8 76438	68.59	51.6 x 20.2		Mud barge, wood, N.R., Reg. to MD&HB 20.2.1877 Vessel broken up. Reg. closed 24.2.1917

H.No. 9 76439	70.24	50.2 x 20.2	Mud barge, wood, N.R., Reg. to MD&HB 20.2.1877 Vessel broken up. Reg. closed 13.11.1895
H.No. 10 76440	55.27		Mud barge, wood, N.R., Reg. to MD&HB 20.2.1877 broken up. Reg. closed 13.11.1895
H.No. 11 76441	65.61	51.8 x 20.7	Mud barge, wood, N.R., Reg. to MD&HB 20.2.1877 Vessel foundered off L'pool Landing Stage Dec 1908. Reg. closed 11.2.1923
H.No. 12 16442	63.60	51.6 x 20.5	Mud barge, wood, N.R. Reg. to MD&HB 20.2.1877 Vessel broken up. Reg. closed 19.4.1923
H.No. 13 76443	69.46	51.2 x 20.1	Mud barge, wood, N.R., Reg. to MD&HB 20.2.1877 Vessel broken up. Reg. closed 13.5.1899
H.No. 14 76444	72.02	51.9 x 20.0	Mud barge, wood, N.R., Reg. to MD&HB 20.2.1877 Vessel broken up. Reg. closed 24.2.1917
H No. 15 76445	65.09	52.4 x 20.6	Mud barge, wood, N.R., Reg. to MD&HB 20.2.1877 Vessel broken up. Reg. closed 24.2.1917
H No. 16 76446	64.47	52.4 x 20.4	Scraping flat, wood, Reg. to MD&HB 20.2.1877 Vessel broken up. Reg. closed 17.10.1907
H.No. 17 76447	54.73	51.0 x 18.5	Mud barge, wood, N.R, Reg. to MD&HB 20.2.1877 Vessel broken up. Reg. closed 24.12.1896
H.No. 18 76448	64.43	51.7x20.2	Mud barge, wood, N.R., Reg. to MD&HB 20.2.1877 Vessel broken up. Reg. closed 26.4.1929
H.No. 19 76449	62.66	51.6 x 20.1	Mud barge, wood, N.R., Reg. to MD&HB 20.2.1877 Vessel broken up. Reg. closed 25.11.1905
H.No. 20 76450	61.07	51.7 x 20.5 x 6.2	Mud barge, Wood, N.R., Reg. to MD&HB 20.2.1877. Reg. closed 3.3.1914 converted to DUMMY BARGE No. 2 re-reg. 3.3.1914. Used at Princes Stage Vessel broken up reg. closed 12.6.1919
H.No. 21 76451	65.82	51.6 x 20.1	Mud barge, wood, N.R., Reg. to MD&HB 20.2.1877 Sold to J.McNaughton for £24. 21.11.1912. Reg. closed 26.5.1913
H.No. 22 76452	52.49	51.1 x 18.5	Mud barge, wood, N.R. Reg. to MD&HB 20.2.1877. Sold to Allan Green of Rhyl, 5.11.1887 converted to steam dredger. Reg. Closed 21.6.1887.

H No. 23 76453	69.28 	51.6 x 20.1	Mud barge, wood, N.R., Reg. to MD&HB 20.2.1877. Vessel broken up. Reg. closed 30.12.1895.
H.No. 24 76454	67.78 	51.2 x 20.5	Mud barge, wood, N.R., Reg. to MD&HB 20.2.1877. Vessel broken up. Reg. closed 31.10.1913
H.No. 25 76455	68.10 	50.1 x 20.5	Mud barge, wood, N.R., Reg. to MD&HB 20.2.1877 Vessel broken up. Reg. closed 25.11.1908.
H.No. 26 76456	66.61 		Mud barge, wood, N.R., Reg. to MD&HB 20.2.1877 Sold to J.McCabe 2.5.1921. Foundered in Hornby Dock Dec. 1933, when owned by Mersey Elevator & Lighterage Co. Vessel broken up. Reg. closed 24.7.1933
H.No. 27 76457	69.77 	51.6 x 20.1	Mud barge, wood, N.R., Reg. to MD&HB 20.2.1877. Vessel broken up. Reg. closed 24.2.1917
H.No. 28 76458	67.11 	50.5 x 20.9	Mud barge, Wood, N.R., Reg. to MD&HB 20.2.1877 Vessel broken up Reg. closed 24.2.1917
H.No. 29 76459	69.28 	51.6 x 20.1	Mud barge, Wood, N.R, Reg. to MD&HB 20.2.1877. Vessel broken up Reg. closed 16.2.1914
H.No. 30 76460	69.59 	51.2 x 20.2	Mud barge, wood, N.R., Reg. to MD&HB 20.2.1877 Sold to Grain Elevating & Automatic Weighing Co. Ltd. 6.3.1913 (£25)
H.No. 31 76461	65.27 	50.0 x 20.6	Mud barge, wood, N.R., Reg. to MD&HB 20.2 1877. Vessel broken up Reg. closed 19.1.1913
H No. 32 76462	71.35 	52.1 x 20.2	Mud barge, wood, N.R., Reg. to MD&HB 20.2.1877. Vessel broken up Reg.. closed 24.2 1917
H No. 33 76463	70.68 	51.4 x 20.1	Mud barge, wood, N.R. Reg. to MD&HB 20.2.1877. Sold to Allan Green of Rhyl, 21.6.1897, converted to dredge gravel
H No. 34 76464	70.96 	51.7 x20.1	Mud barge, wood, N.R., Reg. to MD&HB 20.2.2877. Vessel broken up Reg. closed 16.2.1.916
H No. 35 76465	73.16 	51.8 x 20.3	Mud barge, wood, N.R., Reg. to MD&HB 20.2.1877, Vessel broken up Reg. closed 30.3.1896
H No. 36 76466	70.5 	51.4 x 20.2	Mud barge, wood, N.R., Reg. to MD&HB 20.2.1877. Sold to J.J.Marks (£50) 7.3.1912 Reg. closed 29.5.1913

17

H No. 37 76467	74.07	Garston L&NW Rlwy Co 52.6 x 20.7	1876	Mud barge, wood, N.R., Reg. to MD&HB 20.2.1877 Sold to J.J.Marks (£30) 28.11.1912. Reg. closed 29.5.1913
H No. 38 76468	74.21	Garston L&NW Rlwy Co 52.9 x 20.7	1876	Mud barge, Wood, N.R., Reg. to MD&HB 20.2.1877. Vessel broken up Reg. closed 13.11.1895
H.No. 39 76469	74.29	Garston L&NW Rlwy Co 51.6 x 20.8	1876	Mud barge, wood, N.R., Reg. to MD&HB 20.2.1877. Vessel broken up Reg. closed 24.2.1917
H No. 40 76470	74.07	Garston L&NW Rlwy Co 52.6 x 20.7	1876	Mud Barge, wood, N.R., Reg. to MD&HB 20.2.1877. Vessel broken up Reg. closed 24.2.1917
VIGILANT 76377	269.0 158.0	Liverpool Bowdler & Chaffer 144.2 x 22.3 x 11.9 8 hp. 2 Cyl. eng. J.Jones & Sons, L'pool	1876	Salvage tender, iron, paddle steamer, Converted to lighter 1903. Renamed OCTOPUS.
NUMBER 1. 74500	266.0 158.0	Birkenhead Brassey & Co. 135.4 x 23.2 50 hp. 2 Cyl. eng. Bdrs	1874	S.H.B., iron, s.sc., Reg. 21.3.1876. cost to MD&HB £7.850. Sold to Manchester Ship Canal Co.16.7.1889, (£6,500)
NUMBER 2. 74501	274.0 153.0	Renfrew W.Simons & Co. 139.2 x 23.4 6 hp. 2 cyl. eng. Bdrs.	1875	S.H.B., iron, s.sc., Reg. 21.3.1876. Re named N0.2 8.3.1899. Sold to John Ellis, Manchester 2.9.1910 (£680). Vessel broken up. Reg. closed 21.2.1912
NUMBER 3. 74502	274.0	Renfrew W.Simons & Co. 139.2 x 23.4 54 hp. 2 cyl. eng. Bdrs.	1875	S.H.B., Iron, Reg. s.sc. Reg. 21.3.1876. Re named N0.3 8.3.1899. Sold to Belfast Corp. 9.6.1909. (£1,150) Vessel broken up Reg. closed 31.10.1930.

NUMBER 4. 76488	366.06 156.43	Renfrew W.Simons & Co. 150.2 x 25.2 x 12.4 5hp.2 x 2 cyl. engs. Bdrs	1877	S.H.B., iron, tw.sc. re-named N0.4 8.3.1899. Sold to R.E.V.James Ltd. 15.11.1913. (£1,250)
NUMBER 5. 76489	365.35 155.14	Renfrew W.Simons & Co. 150.2 x 25.2 x 12.3 65hp.2 x 2 cyl. engs. Bdrs.	1877	S.H.B. iron, tw.sc., converted to S.P.D. July 1890. Re-named N0.5 8.3.1899. On hire to Port Talbot Rwy & Dock Co 1909. Sold to Kings of Garston for breaking 1.3.1929. Reg. closed 27.12.1929
NUMBER 6. 76746	365.35 155.14	Renfrew W.Simons & Co. 150.2 x 25.2 x 12.3 65hp.2 x 2 cyl. engs. Bdrs.	1877	S.H.B., iron, tw.sc., renamed No..6 8.3.1899. Sold to Kings of Garston for breaking 1.3.1929. £1,255 for both N0.5 & N0.6. Reg. closed 27.12.1929
NUMBER 7. 78747	366.56 174.14	Renfrew W.Simons & Co. 150.4 x 25.2 x 12.4 65hp. 2 x 2 Cyl. engs. Bdrs.	1877	S.H.B., ron, tw.sc., Converted to S.P.D. July 1890. Renamed N0. 7. 8.3.1899 Converted to water boat to service dredgers in river 20.7.1928. Renamed MERSEY No.7. 22.10.1947. Sold to Abel Barges 13.11.1952 Renamed SAXONDALE 15.9.1953 Vessel broken up 1969.. Reg.closed 4.7.1969
NUMBER 8. 78748	366.22 174.13	Renfrew W.Simons & Co. 15.42 x 25.15 x 12.4 65hp. 2 x 2 Cyl. engs. Bdrs.	1877	S.H.B., iron, tw.sc. Renamed N0.8 8.3.1899. Sold to W.Cooper & Sons 13.9.1943 Vessel broken up. Reg. closed 11.19.1967
OAK 24220	95.78	Liverpool Jesse Hartley 75.3 x 22.3 x 8.8	1836	Ketch, wood, Reg. 24.4.1877. Carried granite blocks from Creetown, Solway Firth to Liverpool for the building of the docks. Sold to A.Cook & A.Galsworthy, general merchants of Appledore 1904. Used as a coal hulk, registration not req. Reg closed 13.6.1904
TOBIN 78822	70.68	Liverpool Thomas Vernon & Sons 99.2 x 21.3 x 10.65	1850	Lightship, iron, MD&HB 26.11.1878. Sold to North British Railway Co. 14.9.1894 Employed as lightship at entrance of Silloth Harbour Sold to R.Abel & Sons Ltd. 31.5.1920. Vesse! broken up. Reg.closed 23.6.1931
PLANET 81325	183.99	Liverpool R.J.Evans 103.0 x 21.2 x 11.6	1880	Lightship, iron schn, Run down & sunk on Formby station 13.8.1921 by s.s. GREENBRIER. Removed to dock for examination after being struck by Currie vessel. RUTLAND 29.12.1931 Sold Van Heyghen, arr. Bruges for breaking 12.3.1964. Reg. closed 14.12.1970

Mersey Docks Fleet List 1850 - 1980

COMET 81351	121.76	Liverpool W.H.Potter & Co. 87.4 x 18.7	1867	Lightship, iron scn, MD&HB 9.6.1880. Run down and sunk on three occasions Raised and repaired each time. 6.5.1895. While on Crosby station struck and sunk by ss EMERALD, raised and repaired 23.4.1898 Crosby station sunk at her moorings when steamer MEDIANA of West Hartlepool ran foul of her. Raised and taken to Tranmere Beach, patched, and moved to No.2 Herculanium graving dock. MEDIANA was outward bound with cargo of coal. Sold to W.G. Wilkie of Morecambe 18.6.1951 for R.N.A. club ship. Reg. closed 10.7.1956 The cost of towing vessel to Morecambe by tug ALFRED LAMEY was £15 more than the cost of the vessel
HODGSON 87849	110.0	Liverpool R.J.Evans & Co 90.0 x 18.2x8.9 80hp.2 x 2 Cyl. Engs J.Jack & Co. Liverpool	1883	Steam Tug, iron, tw. sc. Stationed in south docks as salvage/fire tender, also to keep dock entrances free from congestion at tide times. Sold to Alexandra Towing Co. along with tug NEPTUNE for £10,150 7.10.1920. Both tugs were contracted carry out work they did prior to sale
QUEEN 16867	61.18	West Cowes Michael Ratsey 79.4 x 17.0 x 9.7	1856	No.1 Pilot boat, wood, schooner, MD&HB 8.2.1883. Sank in Crosby Channel 10.5.1891. in collision with ss SAILOR PRINCE raised, repaired and resumed her duties until 1896 when with other of the sailing boats she was withdrawn from service. Sold and employed in the Shetland coasting and fishing trades, early 1900's sold to Faroese, Fuglafjord owners. Wrecked 1.4.1933 at Iceland.
LEADER 17289	60.57	Ipswich Thos. Harvey & Sons. 76.0 x 18.9 x 9.2	1856	No.2 Pilot boat, wood, Schooner, MD&HB 8.2.1883. Withdrawn 1896 Sold to Preston Pilots 15.4.1897.
THE DUKE 16946	62.0	Liverpool W.Buckley Jones 69.0 x 15.7 x 7.6	1852	No.3 Pilot boat, wood, MD&HB 8.2,1883. Sunk in the Mersey by Garston hopper A, raised & reconditioned. Withdrawn and sold to Danish subjects, became a fishing boat
AUSPICIOUS 78804	75.0	Birkenhead Clover Clayton & Co, 82.3 x18.7x 10.0	1878	No.4 Pilot boat, wood, Schooner. MD&HB 8.2.1883. Sunk while lying at anchor at the bar in fog by ss DYNAMIC 17.3.1895
VICTORIA & ALBERT 17770	61.33	West Cowes Michael Ratsey 78.5 x 17.4 x 9.8	1856	No.5 Pilot boat, wood, Schooner. MD&HB 8.2.1883. Foundered at 2.30am on 13.5.1888 being in collision with the barque GOVERNOR in tow of tug STORMCOCK 3½ miles WNW from Bar light, with loss of one pilot
S.R.GRAVES 81314	77.08	Birkenhead Clover Clayton & Co 82.3 x 18.7 x 10.0	1879	No.6 Pilot boat, wood, schooner MD&HB 8.2.1883. Sunk after collision with ss MOORHEN near NW lightship Liverpool Bay 26.1.1896.

LANCASHIRE WITCH
45445   56.05

West Cowes
Michael Ratsey
80.7 x 18.0 x 9.6

1863

No.7. Pilot Boat, wood, schooner MD&HB 8.2.1883. Withdrawn 1896, sold to
Leith owners 11.2.1897.

PRIDE OF LIVERPOOL
42595   74.0

Liverpool
Thos. Royden & Sons
80.0 X 17.6 x 9.7

1861

No.8 Pilot Boat, wood schooner, MD&HB 8.2.1883. Sunk off Point Lynas
by ss RYDAL WATER 2.30am. 26.2.1890. while trying to put pilot on board

SAPPHO
5970   57.0

Gosport
W. Camber
73.3 x 17.3 x 9.9

1853

No.9 Pilot Boat, wood, Schooner/yacht entered pilot service May 1882
MD&HB 8.2.1883. Withdrawn April 1885, sold Feb. 1886 to The British Congo Co.
Wrecked 9.4.1886 on a reef off Colona Point, Bolola River, Gambia.
Reg. closed 17.6.1886.

CRITERION
6001   61.0

Ipswich
Thos. Harvey & Sons.
74.5 x 15.2 x 9.8

1854

No.10 Pilot Boat, wood, Schooner. MD&HB 8.2.1883.   27.2.1892 at 1.30am in dense fog she touched
Middle Mouse off the north coast of Anglesey She put into Amlwch Port for repairs. When repairs were
completed she could not get out of the port as the wind was blowing right in. As pilots were required at Point Lynas
the ENTERPRISE was engaged to convey them from Liverpool and to tow out CRITERION . As she was
approaching Amlwch Port she struck a submerged wreck and had to be beached between the pierheads. 7.12.1895
after being in collision with ss CAMBROMAN off Point Lynas, pilots and crew fearing that she would sink
abandoned her in one of the small punts. The small punt with 16 persons on board drifted for 7 hours before being
picked up. CRITERION did not sink and was towed to Liverpool by the tug CHALLENGER.
Became No.5. in 1898. Withdrawn May 1898 and sold to pilots at Dunkirk.

MERSEY
70945   79.0

Amlwch, Anglesey
Wm.Thomas
80.7 x 19.0 x 10.8

1875

No.11 Pilot Boat, wood schooner, MD&HB 8.2.1883. Became No.3 in 1885.
Sunk by ss LANDANA 2 miles SW of Bar Light vessel 2.12.1885.

PERSEVERANCE
29649

Ipswich
Thos.Harvey & Sons
81.2 x 18.0 x 9.4

1860

No.12 Pilot Boat, wood, schooner. MD&HB 8.2.1883; Became No.9 in 1885.
Withdrawn 1896 Sold June 1898 & sailed to the West Indies to trade between the islands,
renamed WHISPER

NUMBER 9
91161   662.0
             346.0

Renfrew
W.Simons & Co. 1884
185.4 x 33.1 x 14.

1884

G.H.D., iron, s.sc. Renamed N0.9 1899. Sunk in Langton Dock by near miss
from bomb 22.2.1940, salvaged & repaired . Renamed MERSEY No.9 1947
Sold to British Iron & Steel Corp. for scrap 7.2.1957 £12,070.
Arr. T.W.Ward, Preston for breaking 15.2.1957.

ATLAS 91280	456.73 216.86	Newcastle Sir W.G.Armstrong Mitchell & Co. 131.0 X 48.3 X 9.0 40HP. 2 x 2 cyl. Engs Ross & Duncan, Glasgow S.W.L.30-100tons.	1884	Fltg. Crane, iron, tw.sc. Renamed MERSEY N0 39 8.3.1954, name required for new vessel Sold to W.R.Metcalf, Marine Contractor, Bridlington 10.7.1956 Beached at Barrow for breaking by T. W. Ward 22.8.1956. Reg. closed 20.5.1957.
ALARM 91244	223.57 182.16	Liverpool W.H.Potter & Sons 118.8 x 21.2 x 11.2	1885	Lightship, iron, sail. Converted from tw. sc. watch Vessel 1899. Run down & sunk by ss PACUARE 22.8.1911 while on NW station declared total loss. Reg. closed 24.10.1911.
STAR 91281	194.65	Liverpool R.J.Evans & Co. 103.7 x 21.2 x 7.9	1885	Lightship, iron, schr. Run down & sunk by 'EMPIRE SNIPE 7.9.1941 while on Formby station raised 9.9.1941 & repaired, converted to magazine vessel 1950. Sold for scrap 1970, Reg. closed 11.11.1970
MARS 93706	69.66	Runcorn Brundrit & Co. 70.0 x 17.0 x 7.9	1886	Lightship, iron schr. Converted to barge 1912. Vessel broken up. Reg. closed 4.10.1927
NEPTUNE 93789	138.0	Liverpool R.J.Evans & Co. 95.3 x 20.2 x 9.8 80hp. 2 x 2 cyl. Engs D.Rollo & Sons, L.pool.	1888	Stm. Tug, iron, tw. sc. Stationed in Canada Dock as Salvage/Fire tender also used to keep dock entrances clear of congestion during tide times. Sold to Alexandra Towing Co.Ltd (£10.750) see HODGSON. Vessel broken up. Reg. closed 10.3.1928.
TAY 97803	254.48 ---	Stockton Richardson Duck & Co. 125.0 x 23.1 15hp. 2 x 2 cyl. engs. geared.Alex. Chaplin & Co Glasgow	1875	Grain barge, iron s. sc. MD&HB 15.7.1890. Vessel broken up. Reg. closed 14.10.1924.
TAYMAR 90024	65.1	Port Glasgow Blackwood & Gordon 66.1 x 18.4 x 6.9 22hp. 2 x 2 Cyl. Engs	1885	Grain barge, iron, tw.sc. MD&HB 12.4.1890. Vessel lengthened as N0. 14 1894 re.reg. as TAYMAR 17.3.1894. Sold to Wm.Cooper& Sons 23.3.1927. Vessel broken up. Reg. closed 27.8.1959

GEORGE HOLT 102058	109.60	Dartmouth Philip & Sons 101.2 x 21.4 x 12.0	1892	No.10 Pilot Boat, wood, schooner. Sold to Falkland Island Co. 4.8.1904 renamed LAFONIA. Last of the 61 sailing Mersey pilot boats, Hulk in Stanley 1933.
NUMBER 10 102066	231.38 192.02	Antwerp Soc. John Cockerill 124.8 x 24.1 x 8.4 45hp. 2 x 2 cyl. Engs. Bldrs	1884	G.H.D., iron, tw.sc. ex. VOLCANA. MD&HB 23.12.1892. Renamed NO. 10 1899. Sold to Spanish buyers 13.8.1908. (£1,100)
NUMBER 11 102067	231.38 129.62	Antwerp Soc. John Cockerill 124.8 x 24.1 x 8.4 54hp. 2 x 2 cy1 Engs. Bldrs	1884	Hopper, iron, tw.sc. ex. JUPITER. MD&HB 23.12.1892. Renamed NO.11, 1899. Sold to Wm.Cooper & Sons less boiler 26.11.1906. Vessel broken up. Reg. closed 16.5.1948.
BRANCKER 102100	2511.0 1630.0	Barrow, Naval Construction & Arms Co. Ltd. 320.0 x 45.05 x 19.4 225hp. 2 x 3 cyl. Engs. Bldrs.	1893	S.P.D., steel, tw.sc. Dec. 13th 1902 steamer IRISHMAN collided with BRANCKER, at Mersey Bar, dredger received considerable damage to stem and deck tanks. Vessel sold 2.10.1929 (£6.500)/ broken up. Reg. closed 24.10.1930
NUMBER 12 102102	337.85 156.10	Sudbrook Executors of the late T.A. Walker 145 x 27 x 9.0 60hp. 2 cyl. eng. Newall & Co. Bristol.	1895	S.H.B. iron s sc. Renamed NO. 12 1899. Sold to Furness Railway Company 9.3.1906 (£3,150)
NUMBER 13 102123	333.05 144.01	Sudbrook Executors of the late T.A. Walker 144 x 27 x 9.0 60hp. 2 cyl. eng. Newall & Co. Bristol	1893	G.H.D., iron, s.sc. Renamed NO. 13 1899. Renamed MERSEY NO.13 17.10.1947. Sold to Wm.Cooper & Sons 5.7.1951 Renamed NORA COOPER. Vessel broken up. Reg. closed 19.7.1966

WALTER GLYNN 105354	551.0 165.0	Renfrew 1895 W.Simons & Co 189.4 x 35.6 x 12.3 152hp. 2 x 3 cyl. engs. Bldrs	1895	B.L.D., steel, tw. sc., capsized and sank off the north dock wall in 1910, raised and repaired, vessel broken up 1929, reg. closed 12.12.1929
GALATEA 60819	536.0 230.0	Greenock Caire & Co. 219.5 x 26.2 x 13.8 200hp. 2 x 2 cyl engs.	1868	Tender, iron, paddles. Ex. IRENE of Swansea. MD&HB 7.5.1895 Vessel broken up. Reg. closed 2.12.1905
C.B.CROW 105353	2383.53 1522.73	Barrow Naval Construction & Arms Co. 320.0 x 47.0 x 19.42 2 x 3 Cyl. Engs. Bldrs	1895	S.P.D., steel, tw.sc. Sold to Haulbowline Industries, 8.2.1933, £1,500 for breaking. Reg. closed 26.6.1933.
FRANCIS HENDERSON 106814	275.31 ---	Port Glasgow Murdoch & Murray 128.2 x 24.1 x 11.7 3 Cyl. T.E. eng. D.Rowan & Sons, Glasgow.	1896	No.1 Pilot Boat, steel s.sc. Sold to T.J.Kennaugh, L'pool 19.3.1918. Became coastal vessel Vessel broken up on the Clyde 1929. Reg. closed 20.11.1929
SEPTIMA 106808	295.92 244.45	Liverpool W.H.Potter & Sons 95.2 x 24.4 x 13.3	1878	B.L.D., iron To be towed. MD&HB 15.10.1896. Sold to J.J.King of Garston 27.12.1912 (£1,100) Vessel broken up. Reg. closed 7.6.1913
SEXTA 106809	298.71 244.69	Liverpool Bowdler Chaffer & Co. 95.3 x 24.0 x 13.5	1876	B.L.D. iron, To be towed. MD&HB 15.10.1896 Sold to Kay & Dennitts 16.10.1930, £300. Vessel broken up. Reg. closed 13.11.1931.
OCTAVA 106810	295.93 244.45	Liverpool W.H.Potter & Sons 95.2 x 24.4 x 13.4	1879	B.L.D., iron, To be towed. MD&HB 15.10.1896 Sold to J.J.King of Garston 27.12.1912 Vessel broken up. Reg. closed 7.6.1913
SECUNDA 106811	254.36 205.56	Garston W.C.Miller & Sons 93.2 x 24.1 x 12.0	1859	G.H.B., iron, to be towed. MD&HB 15.10.1896. sold to J.Hornby & Sons (shipbreakers) 2.3.1928, for £450. Reg. closed 11.11.1929

Alarm

Atlas

Mersey Engineer

David Fernie, No. 4 Pilot Boat

LEONARD SPEAR Port Glasgow
106825   275.31   Murdoch & Murray
128.0 x 24.1 x11.7
3 Cyl. T.E. Eng.
D.Rowan & Sons, Glasgow

1896   No.2 Pilot Boat. steel, s.sc. Sold to Spanish buyers 1911. L'pool reg. closed 12.12.1911.

LYSTER   619.0   Renfrew
106826   209.0   W.Simons & Co. Ltd.
189.8 x 35.6 X 12.5
152hp. 2 x 3 cyl.
engs. Bldrs.

1896   B.L.D., steel, tw. sc. 18.8.1940 from a near miss in NW Brunswick Dock capsized & sank, salvage started immediately but suspended owing to the loss of salvage gear by enemy action 6.10.1940. Operations re-commenced June 1942, refloated & repaired, served for further 22 years. Sold to T. W. Ward Ltd. for breaking, £3,000. 10.6.1963 Reg. closed 10.2.1964

MILES K. BURTON   Renfrew
106871   1202.32   Wm.Simons & Co. Ltd.
685.91   225.0 x 38.3 x 16.17
2 x 3 cyl. engs. Bldrs

1897   G.H.D., steel, tw.sc. Sold to Arnott Young & Co. Ltd., Glasgow 11.2.1943. £4,000 Vessel broken up. Reg closed 2.1.1950

NUMBER 14   982.44   Renfrew
106894   455.08   Wm.Simons & Co. Ltd.
200.0 x 35.15 x 15.65
2 x 3 cyl. engs. Blders

1897   G.H.D., steel, tw. sc. Renamed NO.14 1899. Sold to Thos. W. Ward Ltd. for breaking, 2.12.1937, £2,450 Reg. closed 15.2.1938

TITAN   256.36   Newcastle
104294   129.88   Armstrong Michell & Co
121.6 x 32.4 x 7.6
16hp. 2 Cyl. Eng.
Cochran & Co., B'head.
S.W.L. 25 Tons.

1896   Floating Crane, steel, s.sc. Renamed MERSEY No.38, name required. for new vessel 19.2.1952 Sold to H.Bath & Sons for scrap, dismantled to water level in Wallasey Dock, beached at Bromborough Dec. 1954 for final demolition. Reg. closed 7.2.1955

QUEEN VICTORIA   Port Glasgow
109416   275.0   Murdoch & Murray
128.4 x 24.1 x 11.7 1
T .E. Eng.
D.Rowan & Sons, Glasgow.

1898   No.3 Pilot Boat, steel, s.sc. Sold to the Guinness family 13.12.1924, became motor yacht ENCHANTRESS   Reg. closed 13.12.1924.

NO.15   982.44   Renfrew
109405   455.08   Wm.Simons & Co. Ltd.
200.0 x 35.15 x 15.65
2 x T.E. engs. bldrs.

1898   G.H.D., steel, tw.sc. Sold to Smith & Houston Ltd, Port Glasgow (£2,600) 2.9.1937, Vessel broken up. Reg. closed 17.2.1938

DAVID FERNIE 275.0 Port Glasgow   1898   No.4 Pilot Boat, steel s.sc. Sold 1937 to Norwegian buyers (Oslo)
109418   91.0   Murdoch & Murray
                     128.4 x 24.1 x 11.7
                     53hp. 3 cyl. eng.
                     D.Rowan & Son, Glasgow

ARGUS   10.13   Barrow   1894   Steam wood, tw.sc. MD&HB 1899. Sold to T.K.Hayes, Liverpoo17.5.1906. Sold to Brandon Bay
110595   2.17   C.L.hair   Salvage Co. London 16.5.1906. Sold to H.T.Ensor, Queenstown, 13.6.1910. Vessel broken up
                     41.3 x 8.8   Reg. closed 19.10.1929.

No. 16   647.53   Renfrew   1900   S.H.B., steel, s.sc. Converted to S.P .D. Feb. 1908. Sold to Haulbowline Ind's. (£500) .
113378   284.31   Wm.Simons & Co.Ltd.   8.2.1933, for breaking up. Reg. closed 26.7.1933.
                     190.3 x 30.1 x 15..6

No. 17   647.53   Renfrew   1900   S.H.B., steel, s. sc. Converted to Welsh Hopper July 1926. (£775) Renamed MERSEY NO.17
113404   284.31   Wm.Simons & Co. Ltd.   18.12.1946, used as mooring hopper. Sold to T.W. Ward for breaking 4.10.1952, £5,000
                     190.0 x 30.15 x 15.3   Reg. closed 23.6.1953.
                     1 x 3 cyl. eng. blders.

No.18   647.53   Renfrew   1900   S.H.B., steel s.sc. Converted to Welsh Hopper 1926. Requisitioned for govermnent service
113416   284.31   Wm.Simons & Co. Ltd.   6.12.1940 no date of return. Renamed MERSEY NO.18 18.12.1946.
                     190.0 x 30.15 x 15.3   Arrived at Cobh 14.1.1961 for breaking at Passage West. (£5,750) Reg. closed 1961.
                     1 x 3 cyl. eng.
                     London & Glasgow Engine &
                     Shipbuilding Co. Ltd. Glasgow.

No. 19   436.56   Sudbrook, Mon   1900   S.H.B., s teel, s.sc. Sold to RG.Odell, Liverpool 1.12.1937. £1,875. Reg. closed 2.12.1937
113371   181.06   C.H. Walker
                     164.0x27.14x 10.79 1
                     3 cyl. eng.
                     Plenty & Son, Newbury

TANTALUS   747.51   Paisley   1901   B.L.D., steel, tw.sc., Sold to T. W. Ward for breaking. Reg. closed 12.5.1927
113444   283.04   Fleming & Ferguson Ltd.
                     190.0 x 38.6 x 13.66
                     2 x 3 cyl. engs. bldrs.

HERCULES 113463	651.61 308.97	Port Glasgow Clyde S.B. & Eng Co Ltd 150.5 x 50.1 x 14.2 2 x 2 cyl engs bldrs S. W.L. 50 tons	1901	Floating Crane, steel, tw. sc. Bombed & sunk in east Langton Dock during May blitz 1941, raised & repaired. Sold to Dutch/Belgian buyers 1970. Reg. closed 14.12.1970
No. 20 113492	703.29 283.65	Paisley Fleming & Ferguson Ltd 190.4 x 30.1 x 14.2 1 x T.E. eng bldrs	1901	S.H.B.,steel, s.sc. Doors altered to carry stone 1940. Burnt out & sunk during May blitz 1941, in No.2 Huskisson Dock, raised & converted to salvage tender, renamed WATCHFUL 11.5.1942. Sold to Panamanian subjects, Reg. closed 13.11.1948,
No. 21 115223	701.66 305.33	Paisley Fleming & Ferguson Ltd. 190.7 x 30.2 x 14.2 1 x T.E. eng bldrs	1901	S.H.B., steel, s.sc. Welsh hopper Sold to Fylde Demolition (£700). 10.4:1941. Reg. closed 15.4.1957
No. 24 115253	434.28 185.41	Sudbrook, Mon. C.H.Walker & Co. Ltd. 164.0 x 27.14 x 10.79 1x T.E. eng. Plenty & Son, Newbury	1901	S.H.B., steel, s.sc. Sold to United Steel Co. Ltd. 29.8.1928 (£1,500). Reg. transferred to Workington.
No. 25 115254	434.28 185.95	Sudbrook, Mon. C.R.Walker & Co. Ltd. 164.0 x 27.14 x 10.79 1 x T .E. Eng. Plenty & Son, Newbury.	1901	G.H.D., steel, s.sc. Sold to T. W. Ward Ltd. for scrap, (£800) 1.4.1927. Reg. closed 22.2.1928
No. 22 115260	700.27 300.58	Paisley Fleming & Ferguson Ltd. 190.2 x 30.15 x 14.2 1 x T .E. eng. bldrs.	1902	G.H.D., steel, s.sc. Cranes removed & converted to Welsh hopper. Renamed MERSEY No.22 21.5.1947. Sold to British Iron & Steel Co 14.6. 1956, arr Preston for breaking 11.7.1956, (£7,500). Reg. closed 14.5.1957
No. 23 115301	700.36 298.06	Paisley Fleming & Ferguson Ltd. 190.1 x 30.15 x 14.2 1 x TE engine Builders	1902	S.H.B., steel, s.sc. Used as mooring hopper for Bucket Dredgers. Converted to Welsh Hopper 1927, (£800) Renamed MERSEY NO.23 30.6.1947. Sold to British Iron & Steel Co 5.11.1956, (£7,250) Broken up at Preston by T. W. Ward. Reg. closed 10.5.1957.

Salvor

Coronation

Samson

Leviathan

CENTAUR 115310	687.77 308.13	Paisley Fleming & Ferguson Ltd 193.7 x 38.15 x 12.2 2 x Compo engs., bldrs.	1902	B.L.D., steel, tw.sc., Sold to Routledge Bros for scrap 13.4.1958, (£4,500). Reg. closed 10.5.1960
OCTOPUS 76777	281.07 276.07	Seacombe Bowdler & Chaffer & Co. 114.4 x 22.3 x 11.9	1876	Dumb Barge, iron. Ex paddle steamer VIGILANT. Converted to watch vessel & renamed OCTOPUS 1902. Vessel broken up as W.S.PATTERSON 1970
VIGILANT 118011	344.48 133.03	Port Glasgow Murdoch & Murray 140.2 x 24.15 x 11.85 2 x T. Inverted Engs. D.Rowan& Co. Glasgow.	1903	Salvage Tender, steel, tw.sc.. Renamed STEADFAST name required for new vessel. Sold to E.W.Fielding for scrap 30.4.1954. Reg. closed 23.8.1954.
EDWARD C. WHEELER Lytham, Lancs 118042	46.27 ---	Lytham S.B. & Eng. Co 65.4 x 14.05 x 8.0 1 x Comp. eng., bldrs.	1903	Pilot river launch, steel, s.sc., Renamed SURVEYOR NO.5 16.3.1921
CORONATION 118050	3034.61 1914.97	Barrow in Furness Vickers Sons & Maxim Ltd. 332.0 x 53.0 x 10.4 2 x T .E. Engs. Builders.	1903	S.P.D., steel, tw.sc., Vessel acquired on behalf of H.M.Government 6.12.1940 used as anti-aircraft ship. Sold by Min. of Trans. to Polimex of Poland and renamed INZ WENDA. MD&HB received £13,000. from M of T. Reg. closed 14.12.1944 Left L'pool for Amsterdam 30.9.1947
VULCAN 118135	789.98 249.21	Port Glasgow Ferguson Bros. 181.3 x 41.15 x 12.35 2 x T.E Engs. Builders.	1904	B.L.D., steel, tw.sc. Sold to T. W. Ward for breaking (£5,100). Reg. closed 13.7.1965.
SAMSON 120916	522.46 345.27	Duisberg E.Bernmhhaus 156.6 x 43.65 x 9.03 2 x Compo engs. bldrs. S.W.L. 30 tons.	1905	Floating Crane, steel, tw.sc. Renamed MERSEY NO.43 to release name for new vessel 26.10.1959 Sold to H.G .Pound, Portsmouth 25.2.1964. Sold to Ass. Elect. Inds. Ltd. London 24.3.1964. Reg.transferred to London. L'pool reg. closed 26.6.1964
GALATEA 120924	588.85 180.47	South Shields I.P .Rennoldson & Sons 170.0 x 30.2 x 13.85 2 x T. Comp. Engs. bldrs.	1906	Tender steel, tw.sc. Sold to Wrightson Bros., L'pool 21.1.1959. Sold to Belgian buyers. Reg. closed 16.10,1959.

ARGUS 120929	29.08 7.57	Liverpool W.H.Potter & Sons 55.0 x 12.6 x 6.45 1 x Comp. Eng. Plenty & Son Newbury.	1906	Launch steel, s. sc. Sold to JH & GH. Potter, L'pool 8.6.1906. Sold to Booth S.S. Co. Ltd. L'pool 15.11.1906, vessel transferred to Brazilian flag 11.2.1908. Reg. closed 11.2.1908
ARGUS 124002	29.36 5.82	Lytham. Lancs. Lytham SB & Eng. Co 55.8 x 12.8 x.6.48 1 x Comp. Eng. bldrs.	1906	Police Launch, steel, s.sc. Sold to Andrew Inglis, Greenock, 27.8.1920 Reg. transferred to Greenock. L'pool reg. closed 30.8.1920
LEVIATHAN 127962	8590.0 5553.0	Birkenhead Cammel Laird & Co 465.0 x 69.3 x 28.9 2 x T.E Engs. 631 hp. D.Rowan & Co. Glasgow	1909	S.P .D., steel, tw. s. sc. Took part in building of Mulberry Harbour during invasion of Normandy A report in *Journal of Commerce* describes her helping construct the artificial harbour at Arromanches,her task was to fill the appropriate parts of the concrete caissons forming the breakwater with sand, to assist them to withstand the winter gales 1.8.1944. Converted to burn oil 16.11.1951. Sold to W. Ritscher & Co Hamburg 1.8. 1962. (£51 000) Reg. closed 8.8.1962.
SALVOR 127963	189.67 94.17	South Shields J.P .Rennoldson & Sons. 110.0 x 25.2 x 9.35 1 x 2 Cyl. eng. 420 hp. builders.	1909	Salvage Tender, steel, s. sc. Renamed STAUNCH, name req;d for new Vessel. Sold to W.G.Everitt of Cork 2.2.1954, £2.600. Reg. closed 24.2.1954.
CAMEL No.1 127972	296.15	Greenwich G.Rennie & Co. 112.4 x 30.25 x 11.0	1909	Salvage Lighter, steel, dumb. Sold to P.Lind & Co. London 11.6..1958, renamed TWEEDLEDEE 30.8.1958. Sold to J.Routledge L'pool 20.12.1971. Sold to Effluent Handling Ltd., Belfast 14.1.1972. Vessel broken up. Reg. closed 7.3.1980
CAMEL No.2 127973	296.15	Greenwich G.Rennie & Co. 112.4 x 30.25 x 11.0	1909	Salvage Lighter, steel, dumb. Sold to P.Lind & Co. London 11.6..1958, renamed TWEEDLEDUM 30.8.1958 Sold to J.Routledge, L.'pool 20.12.1971. Sold to Effluent Services Macclesfield. 12.7.1971. Vessel broken up. Reg. closed 7.3.1980
SURVEYOR 131273	5.2 4.45	South Shields W.H.Rennoldson & Son 30.0 x 7.6 x 3.8 1 x 2 cyl. Petrol eng.	1910	Survey Launch, wood, s.sc. Sold 1936 for pleasure purposes reg. not required. Reg. closed 1.9.1936.
SHAMROCK 95193	83.74	Chepstow C.Finch & Co. Ltd. 85.0 x 17.6 x 9.5 1 Compo Eng. Penarth Slipway & Eng. Co.	1890	Tug, steel, s.sc. MD&HB 1912. Sold to J.Davies, Cardiff 6.4. 1923 (£1,800). Sold to J.Davies Towage & Salvage Ltd. 3.2.1932. Vessel sank in West Dock, Cardiff, raised & broken up. Reg. closed 5.5.1947

31

W.S.PATTERSON Seacombe
76777 281.07 Bowdler & Chaffer.
276.07 114.4 x 22.3 x 11.9

1876 Dumb barge ex VIGILANT ex OCTOPUS Sold to Coopers April 1966
Broken up at Preston, T. W. Ward Ltd. 1970

ALARM 247.23 Leith
135443 Hawthorn & Co.
108.5 x 24.15 x 12.6

1912 Lightship, iron/steel, With steadying sail. Cost £12.165. At first dry docking 14 tons of mussels removed from hull. Sold to Belgians for scrap. Reg. closed 14.12.1970

TREFOIL 121.20 Falmouth
105166 48.44 Cox & Co.
92.0 x 18.1 x 9.4
1 x 2 cyl eng. bldrs

1895 Tender, steel, s.sc. ex HMS FANNY ex OTTER MD&HB 16.7.1912. Used for survey work on Revetment. Sold to Robert Smith & Sons 10.2.1938, £350, vessel broken up. Reg. closed 2.6.1938

FENWICK 160.95 Seacombe
91246 Alexander Jack & Co.
75.1 x 22.2 x 10.6

1885 Barge, wood. Sunk in Mersey, owned by Liverpool Grain Storage & Transit Co. 2.5.1912, raised & registered to MD&HB 13.12.1912. Sold to Abel & SonsLtd 1.11.1950. Sold to Rea Ltd. 9.12.1960. Vessel broken up 1971. Reg. closed 27.8.1971

ALFRED H. READ Port Glasgow
125473 456.98 Murdoch & Murray Ltd.
173.69 140.1 x 27.65 x 12.75
1 x T.E eng.
Ross & Duncan, Glasgow

1913 No.1 Pilot Boat, steel, s.sc. Vessel sunk by enemy mine near Bar lightship, 28.12.1917 Out of 41 on board only 2 were saved, 19 pilots, 8 apprentices & 12 others lost their lives.

ROVER 185.84 Paisley
20452 132.3 x 20.6 x 10.2

1857 Barge, iron, converted from paddle steamer 1889. MD&HB 11.10.1913
Vessel broken up. Reg. closed 15.8.1933

DUMMY BARGE No. 1 Garston
135536 78.33 H & C. Grayson Ltd.
52.4 x 20.1 x 8.8

1913 Dumb Barge, steel, for use at Princes Stage. Reg. closed 18.11.1999

DUMMY BARGE No. 4 Birkenhead
76371 95.38 Thos. Brassey & Co.
75.6x 16.1 x7.5

1872 Pontoon, iron. Converted from lump CONSERVATOR 3.3.1914. MD&HD 14.12.1876 Trans. to MD&HC 1.8.1971. Reg. closed 18.11.1999

SURVEYOR No. 3 Weybridge, Surrey
135543 6.66 Riverside Works Co.
35.1 x 7.35 x 4.2
1 x Paraffin Eng.
Bergius Launch/Eng. Co.
Glasgow

1908 Launch, wood, s.sc. MD&HB 27.1.1914. Vessel bombed & sunk May 1941, NE Albert Dock. Raised & broken up. Reg. closed 19.6.1942

Camel

Vanduara

Mersey No. 4

Walter W. Chambers

DUMMY BARGE No. 2
76450 7   61.07   51.7 x 20.5 x 6.2

Pontoon, wood, for use at Princes Stage. Ex. H NO .20 reg. 1877. Renamed 16.1.1914
Vessel broken up. Reg. closed 12.6.1919

DUMMY BARGE No. 3
76437   64.1   52.3 x 29.6 x 6.15

Pontoon, Wood, for use at Princes Stage. Ex. H NO.7 reg. 1877. Renamed 16.1.1914
Vessel broken up. Reg. closed 12.6.1919

DUMMY BARGE No. 5   Birkenhead   1872
76375   95.38   Thos.Brassey & Co.
75.6 X 16.1 X 7.5

Pontoon, iron, for use at princes stage. Ex lump PERSEVERANCE. Reg. to MD&HB
14.12.1876. Renamed 16.1.1914. Sold 24.10.1960 vessel broken up. Reg. closed 18.11.1999.

CAMEL No. 3   309.84   South Shields   1914
135599   Chas. Rennoldson & Co.
112.3 x 30.17 x 11.45

Salvage Lighter, steel, dumb. Bombed SW Albert dock May 1941 dry docked & repaired.
Trans. to MD&HC 1.8.1971. Sold to Liechtenstein buyers 1977. Reg. closed 21.6.1977

CAMEL No. 4   309.84   South Shields   1914
137391   Chas. Rennoldson & Co
112.3 x 30.17 x 11.4

Salvage Lighter, steel, dumb. Trans. to MD&HC 1.8.1971
Sold to Liechtenstein buyers 1977. Reg. closed 21.6.1977.

VANDUARA   336.74   Partick   1886
93266   216.88   D & W Henderson & Co
169.8 x 24.1 x 14.25
3 x T. comp engs.

No.5 Pilot Boat, steel, s.sc. MD&HB 7.5.1915 Yacht, bought to cover war losses. Sold to
U.S.A subjects, 22.3.1923, renamed FRONTIERSMAN. Reg. closed 27.5.1924

*DANUBE   265.57   Birkenhead   1914
137468   H. & C.Grayson
93.0 x 26.2 x 12.45

Dumb barge, steel, Constructed from part of barge ADRIATIC, cut in halves & rebuilt to
form separate barges. Sold to Liverpool Lighterage Co. 11.10.1950. Sold to Bulk Handling
Services 14.4.1971. Vessel broken up. Reg. closed 12.11.1975

*PLATA   266.73   Birkenhead   1914
137469   H & C.Grayson
93.3 x 26.2 x 12.4

Dumb barge, steel, constructed from part of barge ADRIATIC, cut in half & rebuilt to
two separate barges. Sold to R.Abel & Sons 1.11.1950. Sold Rea Ltd. 1.3.1966.
Vessel broken up. Reg. closed 22.1.1968

SURVEYOR No. 4   8.58   Liverpool   1907
137513   B. Smaridge & Sons
34.5 x8.1 x3.6
1 x Motor
Daimler Motor Co.

Launch, wood, s.sc. MD&HB 1916. Reg. closed 15.11.1930.
Vessel broken up.

Note
*ADRIATIC Off No 113364 440.48 gr 145.0 x 26.1 x 12.3 bt Workington 1900 Dumb barge owned by the Liverpool Grain Storage & Transit Co. Ltd.
After a collision in the River Mersey she was towed to Birkenhead and cut in half & rebuilt into two barges, DANUBE & PLATA.

SNOWFLAKE 41.23 Glasgow 1902 Tender, steel, s.sc. MD&HB 1916. Sold to Liverpool City Council 24.7.1922.
117385 W. Chalmers & Co. Sold to C. Unwin, L'pool 15.2.1928. Sold to R.Munrow, L'pool on same date, renamed JESTER
70.03 x 12.6 x 7.1 5.5.1928. Sold to D.H.Nield, L'pool 3.7.1929. Sold to Port of Dublin 28.5.1930.
1 x T.E eng. J.G. Liverpool reg. closed 28.5.1930.
Kincade, Greenock

No. 1 862.86 Paisley 1916 S.H.B., steel, s.sc. Renamed MERSEY NO.1 18.12.1946. Sold to Van Heyghen Freres, arr'd
137525 406.92 Fleming & Ferguson Ltd Bruges for breaking 13.5.1964. Reg. closed 25.3.1954.
195.35 x 35.56 x 14.45
1 x T .E. eng. bldrs.

CAMEL No. 5 196.16 Leith 1917 Salvage Lighter, steel. Sold to West of Scotland Shipbreaking Co. Troon, for further use
140532 Hawthorn & Co. 18.3.1965 Reg. closed 4.4.1967.
90.1 x 27.6 x 9.75

WALTER W.CHAMBERS Port Glasgow 1917 No.2 Pilot Boat, steel s.sc. Sold to French pilot services. Reg. closed 25.3.1954.
140542 470.16 Murdoch & Murray Ltd.
174.99 145.0 x 27.7 x 12.75
1 x T.E. eng. by
Ross & Duncan, Govan.

ENTERPRISE 132.78 Liverpool 1876 Camel, iron, converted from barge. Re reg. 3.11.1917. Vessel broken up at New Ferry 19
76379 W.H.Potter & Co. 1933. Reg. closed 6.7.1933.
72.3 x 25.3 x 8.9

No. 2 863.01 Renfrew 1918 S.H.B., steel, s.sc. Renamed MERSEY NO.2 22.3.1948. Sold to Belgian subjects (£7,000).
140601 366.35 Lobnitz & Co. Arr. Bruges 30.4.1964. Reg. closed 25.3.1964.
195.7 x 35.65 x 14.45
1 x T.B. eng. bldrs.

IDAHO 42.54 Gosport, Hants. 1910 Steam Yacht, wood, s.sc. MD&HB 3.2.1919. Used as a pilot boat, shortage due to war
128413 21.89 Camber & Nicholson losses Sold to U.S.A. subjects. Reg. closed 19.7.1934.
74.3 x 13.4 x 7.15
1 x T .E. Eng.
Philip & Sons Ltd. Dartmouth.

No. 10 866.48 Renfrew 1920 S.H.B., steel, s.sc. Renamed MERSEY NO. 10 23.7.1947. Sold to Van Heyghen Freres
143623 369.87 Lobnitz & Co. arr'd Ghent 30.4.1964. Reg. closed 25.3.1964.
195.75 x 35.65 x 14.45
1 x T .E. eng. bldrs.

No. 12 143630	743.0 357.19	Renfrew Wm.Simon & Co. Ltd. 189.9 x 30.25 x 15.15 1 x T .E. Eng. Builders.	1920	S.H.B., steel, s.sc. Used as mooring hopper for B.L.D.s. Converted to Welsh Hopper 1926 (£665). Renamed MERSEY No. 12, 7.7.1947. Arr'd. At Preston for breaking by T.W. Ward 31.1.1956, (£4,400). Reg. closed 27.8.1956.
MAMMOTH 143677	1542.0 1033.14	Schiedam, Holland A.F.Smulders 154.3 x88.7 x 12.5 2 x T.E. Engs. N.V.Werf Gusto, Schiedam S.W.L. 200 tons	1920	Floating Crane, steel, tw.sc. Originally ordered by Tsarist Government Sunk by enemy action May 1941, raised & refitted. Sold to Swedish subjects, left L'pool for Oxelosund, Sweden loaded on a barge, 23.8.1986. Reg. closed 18.8.1986. Scrapped 1998.
JAMES H.BEAZLEY 145866	458.87	Dartmouth Philip & Son Ltd. 144.7 x 27.7 X 12.8 1 x T .E. eng. bldrs.	1921	No.3 Pilot Boat, steel, s.sc. Sold to Belgian subjects 1958. Reg. closed 29.7.1958.
CHARLES LIVINGSTON 145885	433.88 156.55	Port Glasgow Ferguson Bros. 144.9 x 27.7 x 12.75 1 x T .E. eng. bldrs.	1921	No.1 Pilot Boat, steel s.sc. Early hours of Sunday 26.11.1939 stranded on Ainsdale Beach, during WNW hurricane force gale bridge and deck houses washed away; 6 crew members were rescued by lifeboat before the vessel was completely submerged, 23 people including 8 pilots and 8 apprentices lost their lives. Re-floated and repaired. During the war served as examination vessel, returned to MD&HB. Sold in 1951 to trade under Honduran flag. Reg closed 19.4.1951.
STIRGIL 140613	52.61 49.61	Workington R. Williamson & Co 51.0 x 17.5 x 6.95	1901	Barge, steel, T.B.T. MD&HB 18.1.1922. Scraping Flat, used for dredging behind lock gates etc. Sold for scrap (£20) to W.Ashton & Sons 20.5.1954. Reg. closed 15.4.1955
STYLUS 140614	52.61 49.61	Workington R. Williamson & Co. 51.0 x 17.5 x 6.95	1916	Barge, steel T.B.T. MD&HB 18.1.1922. Pumping flat, used for dredging around lock gates. Sold for scrap. Reg. closed 15.1.1955.
SURVEYOR No. 2	11.42 5.16	J .S. White Ltd. 45.2 x 9.6 x 4.6 1 x Motor Bergius Launch/Eng. Co	1916	Launch, wood, s.sc. MD&HB 19.1.1923. Sold to Abel & Sons 9.12.1939 converted to a tug, renamed LITTLEDALE 24.1.1940. Sold to Thos.Hodges 10.8.1954.

Mammoth

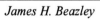

James H. Beazley

Sailing Flat

Hilbre Island

SURVEYOR No. 5 118042	46.27	Lytham Lytham SB & Eng Co. 1 x comp. eng.	1903	steel, s.sc. ex EDWARD C. WHEELER pilot launch. Renamed SURVEYOR NO.5 16.3.1921. Sold to S.A.Portus Garston 5.3.1941. Sold to H.Dillon, Rock Ferry 11.7.1949 Sold to Sandford Repair Co. 10.10.1951. Sold to Standard Lighterage Co.20.11.1951 Renamed SNAPSHOT 17.12.1951. Sold to Snapshot Steam Tug Co. Ltd. 2.1.1952. Vessel broken up 1957. Reg closed 20.5.1957.
BURBO 125648	2963.81 1847.44	Port Glasgow Ferguson Bros. 320.0 x 52.9 x 21.15 2 x T.E. engs. bldrs	1907	S.P.D.,steel, tw.sc. ex LORD DESBOROUGH. MD&HB19.12.1923. Attended D Day Landings on Normandy coast. Vessel sold to T. W. Ward Ltd. (£24,600), arr'd Barrow for breaking 23.9.1954. Reg. closed 2.2.1956
No. 30 147209	892.01 365.73	Birkenhead Cammell Laird & Co 206.9 x 35.55 x 15.35 1 x T.E. eng. bldrs.	1923	S.H.B., steel, s.sc. Renamed MERSEY NO.30 2.5.1947. Sold to Belgian buyers 1964 (£7,000) Arr'd Ghent for breaking 13.5.1964. Reg. closed 25.3.1964.
No. 31 147219	891.78 365.48	Birkenhead Cammell Laird & Co. 207.0 x 35.55 x 15.35 1 x T.E. eng. bldrs.	1923	S.H.B., steel s.sc., Renamed MERSEY NO.31 26.6.1947. Sold to Belgian buyers 1964. (£7,000). Reg. closed 25.3.1964.
ASSISTANT 132080	171.62 16.45	South Shields J.P.Rennoldson & Sons 95.0 x 22.05 x 10.85 1 x Comp. eng. bldrs.	1914	Steam Tug, steel, s.sc. Ex SUNDERLAND. MD&HB 12.3.1924. Sold to J.H.Lamey 31.10.1946. (£1,500). renamed J.H.LAMEY 30.1.1947. Vessel broken up 1962. Reg. closed 4.9.1962.
SURVEYOR No. 6 47249	11.72 6.72	Bangor North Wales Rowlands Dockyards Ltd 38.5 x 9.3 x 4:3 1 x 3hp. Motor Bergius Launch/Eng. Co	1920	Launch, wood, s.sc. MD&HB 8.4.1924. Vessel partially destroyed by fire & afterwards broken up. Reg. closed 4.2.1939.
No. 32 147258	718.11 281.66	Honfleur Chantier et Ateliers 170.95 x 32.2 x 14.15. 1 xT.E. eng. Wm.Beardmore & Co. Coatbridge.	1924	S.H.B., steel, s.sc. Welsh hopper. Renamed MERSEY NO.32. 29.4.1947. Sold to T.W.Ward (£4,500), arr'd Preston for breaking 3.4.1958. Reg. closed 20.8.1958

No. 33 147263	718.11 281.66	Honfleur Chantier et Ateliers 170.95 x 32.2 x 14.15 1 x T .E. Eng Wm.Beardmore & Co Coatbridge	1924	S.H.B., steel, s.sc. Converted to carry stone 1928 (£900). Bombed & sunk in west Waterloo Dock, May 1941 raised & repaired. Renamed MERSEY NO.33 8.8.1947 Sold to Wm.Cooper & Sons Ltd. 1.12.1955, (£7,000), renamed JOHN L.K. 6.2.1957
NO. 34 147274	889.52 364.55	Birkenhead Cammell Laird & Co 207.0 x 35.6 x 15.35 1 x T .E. eng. bldrs.	1924	S.H.B., steel, s.sc. Renamed MERSEY No.34 21.3.1947. Sold to Belgian buyers (£7.000). Arr. Bruges for breaking 12.3.1964. Reg. closed 25.3.1964.
DUMMY BARGE No. 2 147301	99.67	J.Crichton & Co. Ltd. Saltney, Flint 60.1 x 18.15 x 8.65	1925	Pontoon, steel, for use at Princes Landing Stage.
DUMMY BARGE No. 3 147302	99.67	J.Crichton & Co. Ltd. Saltney, Flint 60.1 x 18.15 x 8.65	1925	Pontoon, steel, for use at Princes Landing Stage.
No. 36 148624	772.28 300.23	Le Havre Societe Anonyme des et Ateliers de la Gironde 180.8 x 32.15, x 14.15 1 x T .E. Eng. Beardmore, Coatbridge.	1925	S.H.B., steel, s.sc. Ex FOREMOST 39, MD&HB 30.7.1925. Converted to carry stone 1929, (£1,000). Sank after striking a mine 20.7.1944. Reg. closed 21.6.1945
No. 35 147322	1101.23 465.23	Port Glasgow Ferguson Bros. Ltd. 220.6 x 37.7 x 15.7 2 x T .E. engs. bldrs.	1925	G.H.B., steel, tw.sc. Renamed MERSEY NO.35. 8.5.1947. Sank in Mersey after a collision with tanker FRAGUM 21.1.1955 raised & removed to dock for examination & repairs 8.3.1955. Sold to J.Routledge & Sons 2.5.1955, (£5,755), broken up in Langton dock. Reg. closed 18.7.1956
No. 37 148581	772.25 300.15	Le Havre Societe Anonyme des et Ateliers de la Gironde 180.8 x 32.2 x 14.15 1 x T.E. eng. Wm.Beardmore, Coatbridge	1925	S.H.B., steel, s.sc. Ex FOREMOST 38. MD&HB 13.8.1925. Converted to G.H.B. 1942 Renamed MERSEY NO.37 8.5.1947. Converted to water boat 3.7.1952. Sold to Cooper & Sons Ltd. 8.11.1963. (£7,500), renamed WILLIAM COOPER 13.1.1954. Renamed P.M.COOPER 12.10.1964

SURVEYOR No. 7
135353
15.19 Bangor, North Wales 1923 Yacht, wood, tw.s.sc. Ex DRAGONET of Beaumaris. MD&HB 14.4.1926. Sold to Ross
Rowlands Dockyards Ltd. Maguire, Blackpool, 4.3.1939 Requisitioned by Min. of War Trans. 10.12.1941.
46.0 x 9.5 x 4.9 Reg. closed 11.12.1946
2 x 30hp. Motors
Bergius Launch &
Eng. Co. Glasgow.

ROVER
123990
336.54 Workington 1906 Barge, steel, ex BALTIC of L'pool Grain Storage & Transit Co. MD&HB 1.6.1933.
333.54 R. Williamson & Sons Sold to Liverpool Lighterage 11.10.1950. Sold to Bulk Cargo Handling Services,
131.2 x 24.6 x 11.05 14.4.1971 Vessel broken up 1975. Reg. closed 12.11.1975.

WINNOW
137501
127.16 Groningen 1915 Barge, steel, ex CARBROSIL of Lever Bros & Crossfields, MD&HB 27..1933
124.16 Gerbruden Van Eipen Sold to R.Abell.1.12.1949 renamed CHEEDALE Feb. 1950. Sold to G.Drew & Co. Ltd.
88.4 x 20.55 x 7.05 Oldham 31.1.1966. Vessel broken up. Reg. closed 28.1.1970

HILBRE ISLAND
162374
Birkenhead 1933 S.P.D., steel, tw.sc., Sold to Dutch subjects. Reg. closed 31.5.1962.
3140.5 Cammell Laird & Co,
1807.0 331.7 x 54.2 x 21.1
2 x T.E. engs. bldrs

HOYLE
164253
3137.82 Birkenhead 1935 S.P.D., steel, sw.sc. Sold to In-Situ Cement Ltd., Cardiff. 27.4.1962 (£47,000).
1806.21 Cammell Laird & Co Reg. trans. to Cardiff. Liverpool reg. closed 9.7.1962
331.7 x 54.2 x 21.1
2 x T.E. engs. bldrs

SILO
144876
151.64 Saltney, Flint 1920 Barge T.B.T. ex SILICON. M.D& H.B. 7.3.1935. Sold to Standard Lighterage Co. 10.10.1950
141.51 J.Crichton & Co. Ltd. Sold to Berts Barges 17.11.1955. Sold to L'pool Lighterage 1.12.1958
125.7 x 16.4x7.15 Renamed BEAMING STAR 5.8.1959. Vessel broken up 1967. Reg. closed 17.7.1967

SURVEYOR No. 1
10.63 Wallasey 1933 Launch, wood, s.sc., ex RESEARCH 1 B.A.Southgate, Mersey Laboratory, Dock
6.01 Henry Hornby & Co. Office, L'pool. MD&HB 17.7.1936. renamed SURVEYOR NO.1. 14.3.1956
33.7 x 9.1 x 5.0 1 Renamed SURVEYOR NO 8 10.10.1962. Sold to to R.Richards of Gawsworth Hall,
30hp. Motor Macclesfield, 15.6.1964
The Bergius Co.,
Glasgow.

WILLIAM W. CLARKE
164310
South Bank-on Tees 1937 Pilot Boat No.4, steel s.sc. Sold to Humber Pilots Steam Cutter Co. Ltd. 24.10.1963
579.17 Smiths Dock Co. Ltd. renamed FRANK ATKINSON. Liverpool reg. closed 24.10.1963.
--- 162.5 X 30.2 X 13.25
1 xT.E. eng. bldrs.

No. 24 164334	1104.72 553.69	Renfrew Wm.Simons & Co. 222.1 x 37.7 x 16.5 2 x T.E. engs. bldrs	1937	G.H.D., steel, tw.sc., re-named MERSEY NO.24 18.12.1946. Sunk off New Brighton after collision with MV INDUS 16.2.1956. raised & beached at Egremont, April 1956 for temp. repairs & removed to dock. Sold "as lies" to Westminster Dredging Co. 26.3.1957 (£14,250) Re~named WD54. Liverpool reg. closed 27.3.1957.
No. 25 164345	1104.72 553.69	Renfrew Wm.Simons & Co. 2 x T.E. engs. bldrs	1937	G.H.D., steel, tw.sc., renamed MERSEY NO.25 4.10.1947. Sold to Westminster Dredging, 3.7.1961 (£30,000). Trans. to London register, Liverpool reg. closed 28.7.1961.
TREFOIL 166262	166.68 46.56	The Dock, Northwich W.J. Yarwood & Sons 99.1 x 22.2 x 9.25 1 x Recip. eng. bldrs.	1939	Tender, steel, s.sc. Used for survey work on revetment. Laid up 1956. Sold to Routledge Bros for scrap. 14.4.1960 (£1,500) Reg. closed 9.5.1961. MERSEY NO.37 to carry out as regards Revetment
SURVEYOR No. 4 166286	12.29 5.37	Wallasey H.B.Hornby & Co 31.6 x 9.15 x 5.2 1 x Diesel Eng. J&H.McLaron, Leeds.	1939	Launch, wood, s.sc Last entry in register 1971.
SURVEYOR No. 2 166288	12.29 5.37	Wallasey H.B.Homby & Co. 37.6 x 9.15 x 5.2 1 x Diesel eng. J&H.McLaron, Leeds.	1939	Launch, wood, s.sc. Vessel sold 1962 ?
DENHAM 168810	102.77 35.48	The Dock, Northwich W.J. Yarwood & Sons 71.25 x 18.68 x 10.40 1 x T .E. eng. bldrs.	1941	Survey Vessel, steel, s.sc. Vessel struck a ground mine 18.7.1946 in the Rock Channel, and became constructive total loss. One survivor from crew of nine. Reg cloed 9.9.1946
SURVEYOR No. 6 168842	12.29 5.37	Wallasey H.B.Hornby & Co. 37.6 x 9.15 x 5.2 1 Diesel Eng. J&H.McLaren, Leeds	1942	Launch, wood, s.sc., renamed SURVEYOR NO.9 24.3.1963. Sold to City of Liverpool 5.2.1964
WATCHFUL 113492	719.0 344.0	Paisley Fleming & Ferguson 190.1 x 30.1 x 14.6 3 Cyl. eng. bldrs	1901	Salvage Vessel, steel, s.sc. ex No.20 renamed 11.5.1942. Sold to Greek buyers, left Mersey in tow for Piraeus 19.10.1949 renamed KYRIAKOS

M.O.W.T. 2 168849	614.75 570.86	Chepstow Fairfield S.B./Eng. Co 125.05 x 62.5 x 8.25 S.W.L. 60 tons	1942	Crane, dumb barge, steel, MD&HB 15.3.1943. On loan from M.O. W. T. Returned 20.3.1946
M.O.W.T. 6	614.75 570.86	Chepstow Fairfield S.B./Eng. Co 125.05 x 62.5 x 8.25 S.W.L. 60 tons	1943	Crane, dumb barge, steel, MD&HB 1943, on loan from M.O.W.T. Bought by MD&HB 26.7.1946, renamed FENDER 12.11.1946. Eng. installed for single screw March 1952. Sold to Northern Slipway Ltd Dublin 23.6.1970, converted to twin screw 4.8.1970. Sold to British Transport Docks Board, Hull 6.8.1970. Liverpool reg. closed 6.8.1970.
M.O.W.T. 9 168860	779.34 300.44	Paisley Fleming & Ferguson 173.15 x 57.1 x 10.35 2 x Recip. engs. by bldrs		Floating crane, steel, tw.sc. On loan to MD&HB 1943–1946. Trans. to P.L.A. 1946. Liverpool reg. closed 15.10.1946
ASSISTANT 169313	276.30	Selby Cochrane & Sons Ltd 105.2 x 16.6 x 12.25 1 x T .E. Eng. Amos Smith Ltd. Hull	1943	Tug, steel, s.sc. ex EMPIRE SYBIL. MD&HB 20.5.1946 Sold to Alexandra Towing Co. 16.3.1962. Renamed CASWELL 11.7.1962. Vessel arrived Passage West, Cork for breaking up 25.3.1969. Reg. closed 28.1.1970
BIRKET 168727	777.49 309.71	Paisley Flemming & Ferguson 173.15 x 57.10 x 10.35 2 x Recip. engs. A.F.Craig & Co. Paisley. S.W.L. 60 tons	1942	Floating Crane, steel, tw.sc. Ex M.O.W.T.7 MD&HB 9.8.1946 Sold to British Transport Docks, Hull, 26.3.1979. Reg. trans. to Hull. Liverpool reg. closed 23.5.1979.
MERSEY No. 4 169438	671.0 286.65	Paisley Fleming & Ferguson 162.0 x 33.1 x 14.15 2 x Recip. engs. Barclay Curle & Co. Glasgow.	1945	S.H.B., steel, tw. sc. ex EMPIRE HEATHLAND, MD&HB 1.5.1947 Sold to Westminster Dredging, 2.2.1965 (£9,000) Trans. to London, renamed WD BETA 28.10.1965 Liverpool reg. closed 4.2.1965
MERSEY No. 3 169479	683.19 282.32	Port Glasgow Ferguson Bros. Ltd. 162.0 x 33.1 x 14.15 2 x Recip. engs. J.G.Kincade & Co. Greenock	1946	S.H.B., steel, tw.sc. ex EMPIRE HARTLAND MD&HB 1.5.1947. Sold to Westminster Dredging 2.2.1965 (£12,000) Trans. to London, renamed WD ALPHA 28.10.1965 Liverpool reg. closed 4.2.1965

William W. Clarke

Mersey No. 40

F.C. Birket

Aestus

SALVOR
181106

671.0
246.47
Port Glasgow
Ferguson Bros. Ltd.
164.6 x 34.2 x 15.1
2 x Recip. engs.
J.G.Kincade & Co. G'nock

1947

Salvage vessel, steel, tw.sc. sold to Pemberton & Carlyon (Shipbreakers) Ltd. towed to Garston 29.11.1978 and broken up. Mast and derricks now on road island opposite St. Nicholas's Church, Liverpool, as monuments

MERSEY No. 26
183448

1362.87
612.77
Port Glasgow
Ferguson Bros.
228.0 x 40.7 x 16.9
3 x Diesel engs.
Elect. Drive.
Davey Paxman & Co.
Colchester.

1948

G.H.D steel, tw.sc. Transferred to MD&HCo. 1.8.1971. Sold to Greek buyers renamed TRIAENA Sold to Spanish shipbreakers arrived San Esteban 13.4.1974 in tow from L'pool. Reg. closed 24.8.1973.

MERSEY No. 14
182475

434.77
169.49
Renfrew
Lobnitz & Co.
144.3 x27.1 x 12.15
1 x Diesel, Elect. Drive.
Davey Paxman & Co.
 Colchester

1948

G.H.D., steel, s.sc. Re registered 26.8.1949 on material alteration in breadth to 32.1 ft Transfered to MD&H Co. 1.8.1971. Sold to Cattewater Harbour Commissioners, Plymouth 6.12.1971 Renamed PLYMSAND, Sold to Catalina Properties Ltd. Milford Haven Renamed HAVEN DREDGER. 1986. Vessel broken up 1992. Liverpool reg. closed 24.12.1971

MERSEY No. 27
182482

1262.81
612.77
Port Glasgow
Ferguson Bros. Ltd.
228.0 x 40.7 x 16.9
3 x Diesel engs.
Elect. Drive

1949

G.H.D., steel, tw.sc., Trans. to MD&H Co. 1.8.1971.
Sold to Gerassimos Phetouris, Greece, arrived at Spanish shipbreakers at San Esteban 13.4.1974 in tow from Liverpool. Reg. closed 29.3.1974

MERSEY ENGINEER
183741

749.46
Port Glasgow
Ferguson Bros. Ltd.
181.2 x 41.2 x 12.3
2 x Recip.engs
D.Rowan & Co Glasgow

1949

B.L.D., steel, tw. sc, Sold to Westminster Dredging 2.2.1965. renamed W.D.ATLAS.
Trans. to London reg. Liverpool reg. closed 4.2.1965. Vessel left Liverpool under own power
 March 1965 for Whyalla SW Australia, put into Lisbon for heavy weather repairs left Lisbon for Port Said 13.4.1965, arrived Australia in due course. Vessel keeled over & sank in very heavy weather. 20.5.1966, off Point
 Perpendicular on voyage Whyalla to Sydney: of total crew of 17, 13 were lost.

AESTUS
183744

95.38
30.06
Northwich
W.J.Yarwood
76.8 x 19.6 x 8.2
2 x Diesel Engs.
Davey Paxman & Co.
Colchester.

1949

Survey Vessel, steel, s.sc. Trans. to MD&H Co 1.8.1971. Sold to P .J.Penny, Hydro Surveyor 17.7.1981 Sold to Acecape Marine Ltd. 16.2.1982. Sold to Tamahine Shipping Ltd Ellaston, Staffs, 1985. 18.7.1986 sold to H.Stewart Bracket (Metals) Ltd. Broken up at Birkenhead Register closed 24.11.1999

D. W. Williams

Sir Thomas Brocklebank

Titan

D. W. WILLIAMS 177.18 Northwich 1919 Derrick Barge, steel, s.sc. steamer. Purchased from Brocklebank Line 13.11.1950
143603 100.17 W.J.Yarwood Replaced derrick flat CANADA (122yrs old) Sold to Liverpool Lighterage Co. 5.4.1965.
96.0 x 23.2 x 9.25 Trans. to Bulk Cargo Handling Services 14.4.1971.
1 x Recip. Compo.
engs bldrs.

SIR THOMAS BROCKLEBANK Dartmouth 1950 No.1 Pilot Boat, steel, s.sc. Trans. to MD&H Co. 1.8.1971. Sold to Danish subjects 1976
183794 675.42 Philip & Sons. renamed ODESSIUS as school ship. Last heard of 1984. L'pool reg. closed 10.12.1976.
209.54 140.0x31.6x12.7
2 x Diesel Engs.
Elect. Drive. GEC.
Witton & Nat.Gas
& Oil Eng.Co.

SMEATON 97.0 Northwich 1944 Pumping barge, steel, s.sc. Used for dredging around lock gates ex VIC 33 Built for
168888 42.0 Pimblott MoWT W.D. Army 1947. Purchased by MD&HB from Warnock Bros Ltd. (£5,000) to
66.8 x 18.5 x 8.8 replace pumping flat STYLUS 9.2.1951. Sold to Pounds, Portsmouth 1961
130 ihp. stm eng.
Crabtree

SURVEYOR No. 5 24.43 Southampton 1952 Launch, wood, tw.sc. Trans. to MD&HCo 1.8.1971 Sold to L'pool Polytechnic 2.1.1975
185439 11.45 J.J.Thorneycroft
47.25 x 11.0 x 6.35
2 x diesel engs. bldrs.

TITAN 665.17 Renfrew 1952 Floating crane, steel, s.sc. Trans. to MD&H Co. 1.8.1971. Sold to Greek subjects
185447 254.08 Lobnitz & Co. Ltd. 1973, Reg. closed 24.8.1973
144.75 x 42.0 x 10.3
2 x Stm. Recip. engs bdrs
S.W.L. 60 tons.

VIGILANT 728.39 Southampton 1953 Salvage vessel. steel, tw.sc. Trans. to MD&H Co. 1.8.1971. Renamed STAUNCH
185472 225.05 J.J.Thorneycroft 27.6.1978 to release name for new vessel. Broken up at Garston 1978.
165.0 x 35.1 x 14.75
2 x stm. Recip.
eng. bldrs.

New Vigilant

Atlas

Planet

S.P.D Hoyle

EDMUND GARDNER 185476	700.97 202.43	Dartmouth Philip & Son Ltd. 170.0 x31.75 x 12.4 2 x Diesel engs. elect. drive. National Gas/Oil Eng.Co. Ashton -u-Lyne	1953	No.2 Pilot Boat, steel, s.sc. Trans. to MD&H Co. 1.8.1971. Sold to Merseyside County Council as Exhibit at Merseyside Maritime Museum
DUMMY BARGE No. 6 185497	119.02	Northwich W.J. Yarwood & Sons 69.2 x 19.1 x 12.1	1954	Pontoon Steel, For use at Princes Stage. Trans. to MD&H Co. 1.8.1971. No further entries.
ATLAS 187110	1136.54 513.54	Renfrew Lobnitz & Co. 168.8 x 55.6 x 11.5 2 x stm. recip. engs. bldrs.	1955	Floating crane, steel, tw.sc. Trans. to MD&H Co. 1.8.1971. Sold to Italian subjects 1974. Reg. closed 31.5.1974
SURVEYOR No. 1 187130	12.86	Wallasey Henry B.Homby & Co. 39.4 x 9.75 x 5.0 1 x Diesel Eng. J.J. Thorneycroft, Reading.	1956	Launch, wood s.sc. Trans. to MD&H Co. 1.8.1971 No further entries.
SURVEYOR No. 7 187147	5.35 4.35	Southampton J.J. Thomeycroft & Co. 25.0 x 8.6 x 2.65 1 x diesel eng. geared to 2 Hotchkiss cones	1956	Launch, wood, tw. cones. Vessel sold, no date given Not re - registered.
MERSEY No. 40 187152	1968.10 901.15	Renfrew Lobnitz & Co. 251.6 x 46.1 x 17.8 2 x diesel engs. Rushton & Hornsby Lincoln	1957	G..H.D., steel. tw.sc. Trans. to MD&H Co. 1.8.1971 Sold to West German buyers 1980, resold to Spanish ship breakers and sailed from Brest 10.2.1980 bound for Santander. Reg. closed 24.1.1980.
MERSEY No. 41 187166	1363.85 . 622.77	Port Glasgow Ferguson Bros. 225.6x40.65x15.35 2 x diesel engs. Rushton & Nornsby.	1957	G.H.D., steel tw.sc. Trans. to MD&H Co. 26.11.1971 Sold to J.Willment Marine Ltd 12.7.1984

MERSEY No. 42 187167	636.73 250.33	Renfrew Lobnitz & Co 160.6 x 35.15 x 12.5 1 x diesel eng. Rushton & Hornsby, Lincoln.	1957	Hopper, steel, s.sc. Carried stone from Welsh quarries for revetment. Trans. to MD&H Co. 26.11.1971. Sold to D.Arnald 18.1.1972. Sold to Woodfords, London 2.3.1972. Renamed MERSEY BEAUCOUP 13.9.1972. Sold to Panamanian subject. Reg. Closed 23.7.1976
CAMEL No. 6 187178	650.51 472.80	Port Glasgow Ferguson Bros. 140.2 x 35.2 x 14.9	1958	Salvage Lighter, steel. Trans. to MD&HCo. 26.11.1971
ARNET ROBINSON 187181	734.32 201.84	Dartmouth Philip & Son 170.0 x 31.75 x 12.4 2 x diesel engs elect. drive. GEC Nat. Gas & Oil Eng. Co	1958	No.3 Pilot Boat, steel, s.sc.. Trans. to MD&H Co. 26.11.1971. Sold to Penespy, Formby. 1.9.1982 renamed PENSURVEY 9.12.1982. Sold 5.1.1988 to Gir-Tas Shipping Co. Ltd., Nicosia, used as ferry between Greece and Cyprus. Reg. closed15.11.1989 Still afloat and active 1997. Arrived Alang, India 29.3.2004 for breaking as the FAITH
CAMEL No. 7 187184	650.51 472.80	Port Glasgow Ferguson Bros. 140.2 x 35.2 x 14.9	1958	Salvage lighter, steel. Trans. to MD&HCo. 26.11.1971
SAMSON 301333	773.98 376.35	Renfrew Simons & Lobnitz Ltd. 176.5 x 56.05 x 11.3 2 diesel engs., elect drive. GEC Elect. Co. Ltd. SWL 60 tons	1960	Floating Crane, steel, tw.sc., Trans. to MD&HCo. 26.11.1971 Sold to Zamlift Ltd., Malta 1.12.1987, left Liverpool in tow of former Mersey tug SALTHOUSE ex B C LAMEY renamed ZAMTUG II. On Dec. 12th an RAF helicopter rescued the two man crew from the floating crane after it had parted its tow and was adrift in gale force winds. The SAMSON later went ashore on the Irish coast near Ram Head, after survey it was decided that the cost of refloating the SAMSON would be greater than her salvage value.
DUMMY BARGE No. 7 301335	 100.91 ---	Birkenhead Cammell Laird & Co. 69.0 x 17.8 x 8.5.	1960	Pontoon, steel. For use at Princes Stage. Trans. to MD&H Co. 1.8.1971
PLANET 301353	452.88 291.54	Dartmouth Philip & Son Ltd. 133.0 x 26.6 x 12.6	1960	Light Vessel steel. Trans. to MD&H Co. 1.8.1971. Sold to Trinity House 19.12.1972 then towed to Holyhead. Replaced by a lightfloat with "Dalen" lantern. Reg. closed 10.1.1974

MERSEY COMPASS
303181

2082.89
926.27

Port Glasgow
Ferguson Bros. Ltd.
264.3 x 46.65 x 18.8
3 diesel engs. elect.drive.
GEC & Rushton Paxman.

1960

G.H.D., steel, tw.sc. Trans. to MD&H Co. 1.8.1971. Sold to Dutch dredging contractors Van den Herik Materieel BV of Sliedrecht. Name unchanged. Reg. closed 22.12.1981.

PUFFIN
303861

57.10
23.18

Dartmouth
Philip & Son Ltd.
66.3 x 16.2 x.8.1
2 x diesel engs.
Rolls Royce Ltd.

1962

Pilot Boat, wood, tw.sc. Trans. to MD&H Co. 1.8.1971. Sold to R.V.Coombes 16.7.1979, sold on to W.King same date.

PETREL
303862

57.10
23.18

Dartmouth
Philip & Son Ltd.
66.3 x 16.2 x.8.1
2 x diesel engs.
Rolls Royce Ltd.

1962

Pilot Boat, wood, tw.sc. Trans. to MD&H Co. 1.8.1971.

SURVEYOR No. 3
303866

13.06
4.90

Wallasey
Henry B. Homby & Co
41.0 x 9.7 x 5.3
1 diesel eng.
Gardner Eng. Ltd.

1962

Launch, wood, s. sc. Trans. to MD&H Co. 1.8.1971.

SURVEYOR No. 6
303874

13.06
4.90

Wallasey
Henry B.Homby & Co.
41.0 x 9.7 x 5.3
1 diesel eng.
Gardner Eng. Ltd.

1963

Launch, wood, s. sc. Trans. to MD&H Co. 1.8.1971.

MERSEY INSPECTOR
303878

60.02
28.81

Arklow
John Tyrrell & Sons Ltd.
66.0 x 18.4 x 7.35
1 Diesel Eng.
Gardner Eng. Ltd.

1963

Launch, wood, s.sc.. Trans. to MD&H Co. 1.8.1971 Sold to Cambrian Sea Fishing Enterprises, Rhyl, 2.10.1972. Sold to P.Bowland, Penarth, 21.10.1974. Sold to Aloha Ltd. Gibraltar 14.11.1974, converted to yacht. Sighted in a field near Barcelona, Spain, in poor condition dried out and planking sprung.

MERCATOR 337250	15.28 1.33	Havant, Hants Hull - Halmatic Ltd. 38.9 x 11.0 x 5.3 2 x diesel engs Lister, Blackstone Mirlees Marine.	1970	GRP, Survey Launch, tw.sc. Trans. to MD&H Co. 1.8.1971 Sold to Havelet International Ltd, Guernsey 14.8.1981. Sold to G. Wesley, Milford-on-Sea 6.10.1982. Sold to U.S.A. subjects 1989. Reg. closed 12.4.1989
BISHOPS RETRIEVER 168802	147.49 144.49	Northwich W.J. Yarwood & Sons 87.0 x 20.85 x 8.15	1941	Barge, T.B.T., steel, MD&HB 6.2.1970 from Bishops Wharf & Isherwood Ltd, Warrington Vessel broken up. Reg. closed 6.12.1972
BLENNY 143628	208.08 205.08	Sudbrook, Chepstow C.H. Walker & Co. 94.0 x 25 1 x 11.85	1920	Barge, T .B. T., steel. MD&HB 6.2.1970 from Rea Ltd. Vessel broken up. Reg. closed 7.12.1972
FULMAR 360112	15.73 10.01	Isle of Wight Auto. Marine Eng. 38.6 x 11.1 x 5.0 diesel engs, Cummins Diesels Darlington.	1972	Pilot Boat, wood, tw.sc. Sold March 1985
VIGILANT 378059	817.0 445.0	Holland Scheepswerf "Waterhuizen"BVJ 173.5 x 36.5 x 12.0 2 x Oil engs. 1376 bhp. Rushton Diesels Newton.Le- Willows.	1978	Survey/Buoy Handling Vessel, steel, tw.sc. Left Mersey early 1997 for Talcahuano, Chile Sold to Chilean Naval Mission, for handling buoys in Magellan Straits .
H. M. DENHAM 389187	33.24 20.01	Bromborough, Wirral McTay Marine 53.38 x 21.28 x 6.22 2 Rolls Royce diesel engs	1981	Survey Vess. (Catamarran), steel. tw.sc. Sank after springing a leak while tied up for the night in East Brocklebank Dock, raised and repaired. Owners, 2002 Denham Charters, Liverpool

MERSEY MARINER	Leith	1981	G.H.D., steel, tw.sc., Leased to MD&H Co. from Midland Montague Leasing Ltd.
839177 2720.81	Robb Caledonian S.B.		
	1054.26 257.71 x 52.17 x 18.01		
	4 x diesel engs		
	elect drive		
	Rushton Diesels Ltd.		
	Newton-le- Willows		
MERSEY VENTURE	Appledore	1983	T.S.D., steel, tw.sc. Bow Thrust. Leased to MD&H Co. from Midland Montague Leasing 389224
2605.64	Appledore Shipbuilding		& Foreward Leasing (GB).
781.59	269.86 x 53.74 x 17.03		
	2 x Rushton diesel engs.		
	Newton-le-Willows.		
MERSEY MAMMOTH	Deest Scheepswerf	1986	Floating Crane, steel, tw.sc. Leased to MD&H Co. from U.B.A.F. Bank Ltd.
704483 1764.68	189.09 x 75.32 x 14.83		
582.52	2 x diesel engs		
	elect drive		
	Rushton Diesels Ltd.		
	Newton-Le- Willows.		

O0=0O

Abbreviations

B.L.D.	bucket ladder dredger
G.H.B.	grab hopper barge
G.H.D.	grab hopper dredger
S.P.D.	sand pump dredger
S.H.B.	steam hopper barge

Northwich Guardian, Saturday 12th March 1864.

Launch at Northwich.

A strongly built "mud boat" was launched from Mr. Cornelius Gibson's dockyard on Monday last. This vessel is constructed for service in connection with the dredging operations in the Liverpool docks. Mr. Gibson is building others for the same purpose.

20th Feb.1877

On this day 55 vessels were registered with H.M. Customs by MD& HB.

I discussed this highly unusual block registration with Mrs. McGill the then Registrar of Shipping who was equally surprised. She then made enquiries but found no new legislation or other obvious reason for this occurrence. I am obliged to conclude that the Dock Board was tidying up loose ends.

B.L.D. No.3. wood, sold to Mr. James Heathcock for £180. October 11th. 1889.
Flat LITTLE GEORGE sold to Mr., Daniel Robinson for £7, March 25th, 1892
B.L.D. No.1. sold March 22nd 1897.

MD&HB Fleet in 1905

22	Steam Hopper Barges
2	Steam Tugs
6	Sand Pump Dredgers
4	Cranes
9	Dredgers
5	Derrick Flats
6	Scraping Flats
1	River Launch (Police)
4	Barges for floating hoists
4	Steam Pilot Boats
1	Steam River Launch (Pilots)
4	Steam tenders

July 26th 1929. Welsh Hoppers:- No's 12,17,18,20,21,32,33,36 & 37

When River (sand) Hoppers and Grab Hoppers were converted to carry stone, they were altered to ensure that the opening bottom doors did not extend below the bottom of the ship.

MD&HB Fleet in 1949

77 vessels, ranging from Sand Pump Dredgers to Lightships and from Barges to Salvage Vessels

September 9th 1955.
200,000 tons of stone required to complete the North Training Wall.
460,000 tons of stone required for topping up of existing wall

Mersey Docks Fleet List 1850 - 1980

INDEX

H.No. 1	15	H.No. 24	17	James H. Beazley	36
H.No. 2	15	H.No. 25	17	Lady Sale	14
H.No. 3	15	H.No. 26	17	Lancashire Witch	21
H.No. 4	15	H.No. 27	17	Leader	20
H.No. 5	15	H.No. 28	17	Leonard Spear	26
H.No. 6	15	H.No. 29	17	Leviathan	31
H.No. 7	15	H.No. 30	17	Lyster	26
H.No. 8	15	H.No. 31	17	M.O.W.T. 2	42
H.No. 9	16	H.No. 32	17	M.O.W.T. 6	42
H.No. 10	16	H.No. 33	17	M.O.W.T. 9	42
H.No. 11	16	H.No. 34	17	Mammoth	36
H.No. 12	16	H.No. 35	17	Mars	22
H.No. 13	16	H.No. 36	18	Mary Goldworthy	12
H.No. 14	16	H.No. 37	18	Mastiff	14
H.No. 15	16	H.No. 38	18	Mercator	51
H.No. 16	16	H.No. 39	18	Mersey (I)	12
H.No. 17	16	H.No. 40	18	Mersey (II)	21
H.No. 18	16	Halkin	14	Mersey Compass	50
H.No. 19	16	Hercules	28	Mersey Engineer	44
H.No. 20	16	Hilbre Island	40	Mersey Inspector	50
H.No. 21	16	Hodgson	20	Mersey Mammoth	52
H.No. 22	17	Hoyle	40	Mersey Mariner	52
H.No. 23	17	Idaho	35	Mersey Venture	52

Mersey No. 3	42	No. 23	28	Number 11	23
Mersey No. 4	42	No. 24 (I)	28	Number 12	23
Mersey No. 14	44	No. 24 (II)	41	Number 13	23
Mersey No. 26	44	No. 25 (I)	28	Number 14	26
Mersey No. 27	44	No. 25 (II)	41	Oak	19
Mersey No. 40	48	No. 30	38	Octava	24
Mersey No. 41	48	No. 31	38	Octopus	30
Mersey No. 42	49	No. 32	38	Orion	14
Miles K. Burton	26	No. 33	39	Perseverance (I)	14
Milo	15	No. 34	39	Perseverance (II)	21
Neptune	22	No. 35	39	Petrel	50
No. 1	35	No. 36	39	Planet (I)	19
No. 2	35	No. 37	39	Planet (II)	49
No. 10	35	Number 1	18	Plata	34
No. 12	36	Number 2	18	Pottinger	14
No. 15	26	Number 3	18	Pride of Liverpool	21
No. 16	27	Number 4	19	Prince	14
No. 17	27	Number 5	19	Puffin	50
No. 18	27	Number 6	19	Queen (I)	12
No. 19	27	Number 7	19	Queen (II)	20
No. 20	28	Number 8	19	Queen Victoria	26
No. 21	28	Number 9	21	Rover (I)	32
No. 22	28	Number 10	23	Rover (II)	40

S.R.Graves	20	Surveyor No. 1 (II)	48	Victoria & Albert	20
Salvor (I)	31	Surveyor No. 2 (I)	36	Vigilant (I)	18
Salvor (II)	44	Surveyor No. 2 (II)	41	Vigilant (II)	30
Samson (I)	30	Surveyor No. 3 (I)	32	Vigilant (III)	46
Samson (II)	49	Surveyor No. 3 (II)	50	Vigilant (IV)	51
Sandeel	14	Surveyor No. 4 (I)	34	Vulcan	36
Sappho	21	Surveyor No. 4 (II)	41	W.S. Patterson	32
Secunda	24	Surveyor No. 5 (I)	38	Walter Glynn	24
Septima	24	Surveyor No. 5 (II)	46	Walter W. Chambers	35
Sexta	24	Surveyor No. 6 (I)	38	Watchful	41
Shamrock	31	Surveyor No. 6 (II)	41	Wellington	12
Sidney	14	Surveyor No. 6 (III)	50	William W. Clarke	40
Silo	40	Surveyor No. 7 (I)	40	Winnow	40
Sir Thomas Brocklebank	46	Surveyor No. 7 (II)	48		
Sirius	14	Tantalus	27		
Smeaton	46	Tay	22		
Snowflake	35	Taymar	22		
Spitfire	15	The Duke	20		
Star	22	Titan (I)	26		
Stirgil	36	Titan (II)	46		
Stylus	36	Tobin	19		
Surveyor	31	Trefoil	41		
Surveyor No. 1 (I)	40	Vanduara	34		

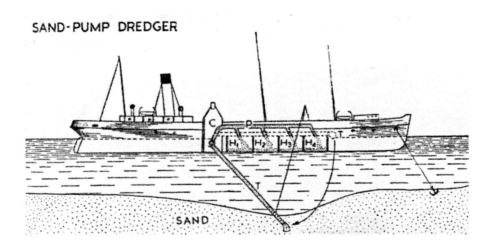

SAND-PUMP DREDGER

SAND